THE USES OF DIVERSITY

A Book of Essays

by

G. K. CHESTERTON

First Published in 1920

NATAL PUBLISHING LLC
ARS LONGA, VITA BREVIS

Copyright© 2024 Natal Publishing

All rights reserved

Cover art by Mauricio A. on Pixabay

CONTENTS

THE PLAN FOR A NEW UNIVERSE

GEORGE WYNDHAM

FOUR STUPIDITIES

ON HISTORICAL NOVELS

ON MONSTERS

Transcriber's Notes: 1. Obvious printer's errors corrected. 2. Every effort has been made to replicate this text as faithfully as possible, including obsolete and variant spellings, non-standard punctuation, inconsistently hyphenated words, and other inconsistencies, e.g. George Sand's name is misprinted as "Georges Sand." Left as printed.

On Seriousness

I DO not like seriousness. I think it is irreligious. Or, if you prefer the phrase, it is the fashion of all false religions. The man who takes everything seriously is the man who makes an idol of everything: he bows down to wood and stone until his limbs are as rooted as the roots of the tree or his head as fallen as the stone sunken by the roadside. It has often been discussed whether animals can laugh. The hyena is said to laugh: but it is rather in the sense in which the M.P. is said to utter "an ironical cheer." At the best, the hyena utters an ironical laugh. Broadly, it is true that all animals except Man are serious. And I think it is further demonstrated by the fact that all human beings who concern themselves in a concentrated way with animals are also serious; serious in a sense far beyond that of human beings concerned with anything else. Horses are serious; they have long, solemn faces. But horsey men are also serious—jockeys or trainers or grooms: they also have long, solemn faces. Dogs are serious: they have exactly that combination of moderate conscientiousness with monstrous conceit which is the make-up of most modern religions. But, however serious dogs may be, they can hardly be more serious than dog-fanciers—or dog-stealers. Dog-stealers, indeed, have to be particularly serious, because they have to come back and say they have found the dog. The faintest shade of irony, not to say levity, on their features, would evidently be fatal to their plans. I will not carry the comparison through all the kingdoms of natural history: but it is true of all who fix their affection or intelligence on the lower animals. Cats are as serious as the Sphinx, who must have been some kind of cat, to judge by the attitude. But the rich old ladies who love cats are quite equally serious, about cats and about themselves. So also the ancient Egyptians worshipped cats, also crocodiles and beetles and all kinds of things; but they were all serious and made their worshippers serious. Egyptian art was intentionally harsh, clear, and conventional; but it could very vividly represent men driving, hunting, fighting, feasting, praying. Yet I think you will pass along many corridors of that coloured and almost cruel art before you see a man laughing. Their gods did not encourage them to laugh. I am told by housewives that beetles seldom laugh. Cats do not laugh—except the Cheshire Cat (which is not found in Egypt); and even he can only grin. And crocodiles do not laugh. They weep.

This comparison between the sacred animals of Egypt and the pet animals of to-day is not so far-fetched as it may seem to some people. There is a healthy and an unhealthy love of animals: and the nearest definition of the difference is that the unhealthy love of animals is serious. I am quite prepared to love a rhinoceros, with reasonable precautions: he is, doubtless, a delightful father to the young rhinoceroses. But I will not promise not to laugh at a rhinoceros. I will not worship the beast with the little horn. I will not adore the Golden Calf; still less will I adore the Fatted Calf. On the contrary, I will eat him. There is some sort of joke about eating an animal, or even about an animal eating you. Let us hope we shall perceive it at the proper moment, if it ever occurs. But I will not worship an animal. That is, I will not take an animal quite seriously: and I know why.

Wherever there is Animal Worship there is Human Sacrifice. That is, both symbolically and literally, a real truth of historical experience. Suppose a thousand black slaves were sacrificed to the blackbeetle; suppose a million maidens were flung into the Nile to feed the crocodile; suppose the cat could eat men instead of mice—it could still be no more than that sacrifice of humanity that so often makes the horse more important than the groom, or the lap-dog more important even than the lap. The only right view of the animal is the comic view. Because the view is comic it is naturally affectionate. And because it is affectionate, it is never respectful.

I know no place where the true contrast has been more candidly, clearly, and (for all I know) unconsciously expressed than in an excellent little book of verse called *Bread and Circuses* by Helen Parry Eden, the daughter of Judge Parry, who has inherited both the humour and the humanity in spite of which her father succeeded as a modern magistrate. There are a great many other things that might be praised in the book, but I should select for praise the sane love of animals. There is, for instance, a little poem on a cat from the country who has come to live in a flat in Battersea (everybody at some time of their lives has lived or will live in a flat in Battersea, except, perhaps, the "prisoner of the Vatican"), and the verses have a tenderness, with a twist of the grotesque, which seems to me the exactly appropriate tone about domestic pets:

> And now you're here. Well, it may be
> The sun *does* rise in Battersea
> Although to-day be dark;
> Life is not shorn of loves and hates
> While there are sparrows on the slates
> And keepers in the Park.
> And you yourself will come to learn
> The ways of London; and in turn
> Assume your Cockney cares
> Like other folk that live in flats,
> Chasing your purely abstract rats
> Upon the concrete stairs.

That is like Hood at his best; but it is, moreover, penetrated with a profound and true appreciation of the fundamental idea that all love of the cat must be founded on the *absurdity* of the cat, and only thus can a morbid idolatry be avoided. Perhaps those who appeared to be witches were those old ladies who took their cats too seriously. The cat in this book is called "Four-Paws," which is as jolly as a gargoyle. But the name of the cat must be something familiar and even jeering, if it be only Tom or Tabby or Topsy: something that shows man is not afraid of it. Otherwise the name of the cat will be Pasht.

But when the same poet comes accidentally across an example of the insane seriousness about animals that some modern "humanitarians" exhibit, she turns against the animal-lover as naturally and instinctively as she turns to the animal. A writer on a society paper had mentioned some rich woman who had appeared on Cup Day "gowned" in some way or other, and inserted the tearful parenthesis that "she has just lost a dear dog in London." The real animal-lover instantly recognizes the wrong note, and dances on the dog's grave with a derision as unsympathetic as Swift:

> Dear are my friends, and yet my heart still light is,
>> Undimmed the eyes that see our set depart,
> Snatched from the Season by appendicitis
>> Or something quite as smart.
> But when my Chin-Chin drew his latest breath

> On Marie's outspread apron, slow and wheezily,
> I simply sniffed, I could not take *his* death
> So Pekineasily....
> ... Grief courts these ovations,
> And many press my sable-suèded hand,
> Noting the blackest of Lucile's creations
> Inquire, and understand.

It is that balance of instincts that is the essence of all satire: however fantastic satire may be, it must always be potentially rational and fundamentally moderate, for it must be ready to hit both to right and to left at opposite extravagances. And the two extravagances which exist on the edges of our harassed and secretive society to-day are cruelty to animals and worship of animals. They both come from taking animals too seriously: the cruel man must hate the animal; the crank must worship the animal, and perhaps fear it. Neither knows how to love it.

Lamp-Posts

IN contemplating some common object of the modern street, such as an omnibus or a lamp-post, it is sometimes well worth while to stop and think about why such common objects are regarded as commonplace. It is well worth while to try to grasp what is the significance of them—or rather, the quality in modernity which makes them so often seem not so much significant as insignificant. If you stop the omnibus while you stop to think about it, you will be unpopular. Even if you try to grasp the lamp-post in your effort to grasp its significance, you will almost certainly be misunderstood. Nevertheless, the problem is a real one, and not without bearing upon the most poignant politics and ethics of to-day. It is certainly not the things themselves, the idea and upshot of them, that are remote from poetry or even mysticism. The idea of a crowd of human strangers turned into comrades for a journey is full of the oldest pathos and piety of human life. That profound feeling of mortal fraternity and frailty, which tells us we are indeed all in the same boat, is not the less true if expressed in the formula that we are all in the same bus. As for the idea of the lamp-post, the idea of the fixed beacon of the branching thoroughfares, thc terrestrial star of the terrestrial traveller, it not only could be, but actually is, the subject of countless songs.

Nor is it even true that there is something so trivial or ugly about the names of the things as to make them commonplace in all connexions. The word "lamp" is especially beloved by the more decorative and poetic writers; it is a symbol, and very frequently a title. It is true that if Ruskin had called his eloquent work "The Seven Lamp-Posts of Architecture" the effect, to a delicate ear, would not have been quite the same. But even the word "post" is in no sense impossible in poetry; it can be found with a fine military ring in phrases like "The Last Post" or "Dying at his Post." I remember, indeed, hearing, when a small child, the line in Macaulay's "Armada" about "with loose rein and bloody spur rode inland many a post," and being puzzled at the picture of a pillar-box or a lamp-post displaying so much activity. But certainly it is not the mere sound of the word that makes it unworkable in the literature of wonder or beauty. "Omnibus" may seem at first sight a more difficult thing to swallow—if I may be allowed a somewhat gigantesque figure of speech. This, it may be said, is a Cockney and ungainly modern word, as it is certainly a Cockney and ungainly modern thing. But even this is not true. The word "omnibus" is a very noble word with a very noble meaning and even tradition. It is derived from an ancient and adamantine tongue which has rolled it with very authoritative thunders: *quod ubique, quod semper, quod ab omnibus*. It is a word really more human and universal than republic or democracy. A man might very consistently build a temple for all the tribes of men, a temple of the largest pattern and the loveliest design, and then call it an omnibus. It is true that the dignity of this description has really been somewhat diminished by the illogical habit of clipping the word down to the last and least important part of it. But that is only one of many modern examples in which real vulgarity is not in democracy, but rather in the loss of democracy. It is about as democratic to call an omnibus a bus as it would be to call a democrat a rat.

Another way of explaining the cloud of commonplace interpretation upon modern things is to trace it to that spirit which often calls itself science but which is more often mere repetition. It is proverbial that a child, looking out of the nursery window, regards the lamp-post as part of a fairy-tale of which the lamplighter is the fairy. That lamp-post can be to a baby all that the moon could possibly be to a lover or a poet. Now, it is perfectly true that there is nowadays a spirit of cheap information which imagines that it shoots beyond this shining point, when it merely tells us that there are nine hundred lamp-posts in the town, all exactly alike. It is equally true that there is a spirit of cheap science, which is equally cocksure of its conclusiveness when it tells us that there are so many thousand moons and suns, all much more alike than we might have been disposed to fancy. And we can say of both these calculations that there is nothing really commonplace except the mind of the calculator. The baby is much more right about the flaming lamp than the statistician who counts the posts in the street; and the lover is much more really right about the moon than the astronomer. Here the part is certainly greater than the whole, for it is much better to be tied to one wonderful thing than to allow a mere catalogue of wonderful things to deprive you of the capacity to wonder. It is doubtless true, to a definite extent, that a certain sameness in the mechanical modern creations makes them actually less attractive than the freer recurrences of nature; or, in other words, that twenty lamp-posts really are much more like each other than twenty trees. Nevertheless, even this character will not cover the whole ground, for men do not cease to feel the mystery of natural things even when they reproduce themselves almost completely, as in the case of pitch darkness or a very heavy sleep. The mere fact that we have seen a lamp-post very often, and that it generally looked very much the same as before, would not of itself prevent us from appreciating its elfin fire, any more than it prevents the child.

Finally, there is a neglected side of this psychological problem which is, I think, one aspect of the mystery of the morality of war. It is not altogether an accident that, while the London lamp-post has always been mild and undistinguished, the Paris lamp-post has been more historic because it has been more horrible. It has been a yet more revolutionary substitute for the guillotine—yet more revolutionary, because it was the guillotine of the mob, as distinct even from the guillotine of the Republic. They hanged aristocrats upon it, including (unless my memory misleads me) that exceedingly unpleasant aristocrat who promulgated the measure of war economy known as "Let them eat grass." Hence it happened that there has been in Paris a fanatical and flamboyant political newspaper actually called *La Lanterne*, a paper for extreme Jacobins. If there were a paper in London called the *Lamp-Post*, I can only imagine it as a paper for children. As for my other example, I do not know whether even the French Revolution could manage to do anything with the omnibus; but the Jacobins were quite capable of using it as a tumbril.

In short, I suspect that Cockney things have become commonplace because there has been so long lacking in them a certain savour of sacrifice and peril, which there has been in the nursery tale, for all its innocence, and which there has been in the Parisian street, for all its iniquity.

The new wonder that has changed the world before our eyes is that all this crude and vulgar modern clockwork is most truly being used for a heroic end. It is most emphatically being used for the slaying of a dragon. It is being used, much more unquestionably than the lantern of Paris, to make an end of a tyrant. It was a cant phrase in our cheaper literature of late to say that the new time will make the romance of war mechanical. Is it not more probable that it will make the mechanism of war romantic? As I said at the beginning, the things themselves are not repulsively prosaic; it was their associations that made them so; and to-day their associations are as splendid as any that ever blazoned a shield or embroidered a banner. Much of what made the violation of Belgium so violent a challenge to every conscience lay unconsciously in the fact that the country which had thus become tragic had often been regarded as commonplace. The unpardonable sin was committed in a place of lamp-posts and omnibuses. In similar places has been prepared the just wrath and reparation; and a legend of it will surely linger even in the omnibus that has carried heroes to the mouth of hell, and even in the lamp-post whose lamp has been darkened against the dragon of the sky.

The Spirits

THE magazines continue to abound in articles about Spiritualism. Those articles which expose and explode Spiritualism are certainly calculated to make converts to that novel creed; but fortunately the balance is redressed by the articles which defend and expound Spiritualism, which will probably make any thoughtful convert hastily recant his conversion. I believe myself that nothing but advantage can accrue to Spiritualism from all criticisms founded on Materialism. I think there is a mystical minimum in human history and experience, which is at once too obscure to be explained and too obvious to be explained away. It may be admitted that a miracle is rarer than a murder; but they are made obscure by somewhat similar causes. Thus a medium will insist on a dark room; and a murderer is said to have a slight preference for a dark night. A medium is criticized for not submitting to a sufficient number of scientific and impartial judges; and a murderer seldom collects any considerable number of impartial witnesses to testify to his performance. Many supernatural stories rest on the evidence of rough unlettered men, like fishermen and peasants; and most criminal trials depend on the detailed testimony of quite uneducated people. It may be remarked that we never throw a doubt on the value of ignorant evidence when it is a question of a judge hanging a man, but only when it is a question of a saint healing him. Morbid and hysterical people imagine all sorts of ghosts and demons that do not exist. Morbid and hysterical people also imagine all sorts of crimes and conspiracies that do not exist. A great many spiritual communications may be auto-suggestions; and a great many apparent murders may be suicides. But there is a limit to the probability of self-destruction; so there is of self-deception.

Now I think it well worth while to concentrate our common sense, not on where these messages come from, or why they come, but simply on the messages. Let us consider the thing itself about which there is no doubt at all. Let us consider, not whether spirits can speak to us, or how they speak, but simply what they say, or are supposed to say. If spirits in heaven, or scoundrels on earth, or fiends somewhere else, have brought us a new religion, let us look at the new religion on its own merits. Well, this is the sort of thing the spirits are supposed to write down, and very possibly do write down:

"You make death an impenetrable fog, while it is a mere golden mist, torn easily aside by the shafts of faith, and revealing life as not only continuous but as not cut in two by a great change. I cannot express myself as I wish.... It is more like leaving prison for freedom and happiness. Not that your present life lacks joy; it is all joy, but you have to fight with imperfections. Here, we have to struggle only with lack of development. There is no evil—only different degrees of spirit."

The interrogator, Mr. Basil King, who narrates his experiences in an interesting article in *Nash's Magazine*, proceeds to ask whether the lack of development is due to the highly practical thing we call sin. To this the spirit replies: "They come over with the evil, as it were, cut out, and leaving blanks in their souls. These have by degrees to be filled with good."

Now I will waive the point whether death is a mist or a fog or a front door or a fire-escape or any other physical metaphor; being satisfied with the fact that it is there, and not to be removed by metaphors. But what amuses me about the spirit is that for him it is both there and not there. Death is non-existent in one sentence, and of the most startling importance six sentences afterwards. The spirit is positive that our existence is *not* cut in two by a great change, at the moment of death. But the spirit is equally positive, a little lower down, that the whole of our human evil is instantly and utterly cut out of us, and all at the moment of death. If a man suddenly and supernaturally loses about three-quarters of his ordinary character, might it not be described as "a great change"? Why does so enormous a convulsion happen at the exact moment of death, if death is non-existent and not to be considered? The Spiritualist is here contradicting himself, not only by making death very decidedly a great change, but by actually making it a greater change than Dante or St. Francis thought it was. A Christian who thinks the soul carries its sins to Purgatory makes life much more "continuous" than this Spiritualist, who says that death, and death alone, alters a man as by a blast of magic. The article bears the modest title of "The Abolishing of Death"; and the spirit does say that this is possible, except when he forgets and says the opposite. He seldom contradicts himself more than twice in a paragraph. But since he says clearly that death abolishes sin, and equally clearly that he abolishes death, it becomes an interesting speculation what happens next, and especially what happens to sin: a subject of interest to many of us.

Mr. Basil King asked the spirit, who had told him that animals are human, whether it is wrong to destroy animal life. It may be remarked that the questions Mr. King asks are always much more acute than the answers he gets. The answer about the killing of animals is this: "You can *never* destroy life. Life is the absolute power which overrules all else. There can be no cessation. It is impossible." And that is all; and for a man considering whether he shall or shall not kill a tom-cat, it does not seem very helpful. Logically, if it means anything, it would seem to mean that you may do anything to the cat, for its nine lives are really an infinite series. In short, you can kill it because you cannot kill it. But it is obvious that if a man relies on this reason for killing his cat, it is an equally good reason for killing his creditor. Creditors also are immortal (a solemn thought); creditors also pass through a golden mist torn easily aside by the shafts of faith, and have all the evil of their souls (including, let us hope, their avarice) cut out of them with the axe of death, without noticing anything in particular. In short, Mr. Basil King, when he asks a reasonable question about a real moral question, the relations of man and the animals, gets no reply except a hotch-potch of words which might mean anarchy and may mean anything. From beginning to end the spirit never answers any real question on which the real religions of mankind have been obliged to legislate and to teach. The only practical deduction would be that it is *no* disadvantage to have sinned in this life; as in the other case that it is *no* disgrace to kill either a creditor or a cat. If it means anything, it means that; and if it is spirits and not spifflications, the spirits mean that: and I do not desire their further acquaintance.

Tennyson

I HAVE been glancing over two or three of the appreciations of Tennyson appropriate to his centenary, and have been struck with a curious tone of coldness towards him in almost all quarters. Now this is really a very peculiar thing. For it is a case of coldness to quite brilliant and unquestionable literary merit. Whether Tennyson was a great poet I shall not discuss. I understand that one has to wait about eight hundred years before discussing that; and my only complaint against the printers of my articles is that they will not wait even for much shorter periods. But that Tennyson was a poet is as solid and certain as that Roberts is a billiard-player. That Tennyson was an astonishingly good poet is as solid and certain as that Roberts is an astonishingly good billiard-player. Even in these matters of art there are some things analogous to matters of fact. It is no good disputing about tastes—partly because some tastes are beyond dispute. If anyone tells me that

> There is fallen a splendid tear
>
> From the passion-flower at the gate;
>
> or that
>
> Tears from the depth of some divine despair

is not fine poetry, I am quite prepared to treat him as I would one who said that grass was not green or that I was not corpulent. And by all common chances Tennyson ought to be preserved as a pleasure—a sensuous pleasure if you like, but certainly a genuine one. There is no more reason for dropping Tennyson than for dropping Virgil. We do not mind Virgil's view of Augustus, nor need we mind Tennyson's view of Queen Victoria. Beauty is unanswerable, in a poem as much as in a woman. There were Victorian writers whose art is not perfectly appreciable apart from their enthusiasm. Kingsley's *Yeast* is a fine book, but not quite so fine a book as it seemed when one's own social passions were still yeasty. Browning and Coventry Patmore are justly admired, but they are most admired where they are most agreed with. But "St. Agnes' Eve" is an unimpeachably beautiful poem, whether one believes in St. Agnes or detests her. One would think that a man who had thus left indubitably good verse would receive natural and steady gratitude, like a man who left indubitably good wine to his nephew, or indubitably good pictures to the National Portrait Gallery. Nevertheless, as I have said, the tone of all the papers, modernist or old-fashioned, has been mainly frigid. What is the meaning of this?

I will ask permission to answer this question by abruptly and even brutally changing the subject. My remarks must, first of all, seem irrelevant even to effrontery; they shall prove their relevance later on. In turning the pages of one of the papers containing such a light and unsympathetic treatment of Tennyson, my eye catches the following sentence: "By the light of modern science and thought, we are in a position to see that each normal human being in some way repeats historically the life of the human race." This is a very typical modern assertion; that is, it is an assertion for which there is not and never has been a single spot or speck of proof. We know precious little about what the life of the human race has been; and none of our scientific conjectures about it bear the remotest resemblance to the actual growth of a child. According to this theory, a baby begins by chipping flints and rubbing sticks together to find fire. One so often sees babies doing this. About the age of five the child, before the delighted eyes of his parents, founds a village community. By the time he is eleven it has become a small city state, the replica of ancient Athens. Encouraged by this, the boy proceeds, and before he is fourteen has founded the Roman Empire. But now his parents have a serious set-back. Having watched him so far, not only with pleasure, but with a very natural surprise, they must strengthen themselves to endure the spectacle of decay. They have now to watch their child going through the decline of the Western Empire and the Dark Ages. They see the invasion of the Huns and that of the Norsemen chasing each other across his expressive face. He seems a little happier after he has "repeated" the Battle of Chalons and the unsuccessful Siege of Paris; and by the time he comes to the twelfth century, his boyish face is as bright as it was of old when he was "repeating" Pericles or Camillus. I have no space to follow this remarkable demonstration of how history repeats itself in the youth; how he grows dismal at twenty-three to represent the end of Mediævalism, brightens because the Renaissance is coming, darkens again with the disputes of the later Reformation, broadens placidly through the thirties as the rational eighteenth century, till at last, about forty-three, he gives a great yell and begins to burn the house down, as a symbol of the French Revolution. Such (we shall all agree) is the ordinary development of a boy.

Now, seriously, does anyone believe a word of such bosh? Does anyone think that a child will repeat the periods of human history? Does anyone ever allow for a daughter in the Stone Age, or excuse a son because he is in the fourth century B.C. Yet the writer who lays down this splendid and staggering lie calmly says that "by the light of modern science and thought we are in a position to *see*" that it is true. "Seeing" is a strong word to use of our conviction that icebergs are in the north, or that the earth goes round the sun. Yet anybody can use it of any casual or crazy biological fancy seen in some newspaper or suggested in some debating club. This is the rooted weakness of our time. Science, which means exactitude, has become the mother of all inexactitude.

This is the failure of the epoch, and this explains the partial failure of Tennyson. He was *par excellence* the poet of popular science—that is, of all such cloudy and ill-considered assertions as the above. He was the perfectly educated man of classics and the half-educated man of science. No one did more to encourage the colossal blunder that the survival of the fittest means the survival of the best. One might as well say that the survival of the fittest means the survival of the fattest. Tennyson's position has grown shaky because it rested not on any clear dogmas old or new, but on two or three temporary, we might say desperate, compromises of his own day. He grasped at Evolution, not because it was definite, but because it was indefinite; not because it was daring, but because it was safe. It gave him the hope that man might one day be an angel, and England a free democracy; but it soothed him with the assurance that neither of these alarming things would happen just yet. Virgil used his verbal felicities to describe the eternal idea of the Roman Imperium. Tennyson used his verbal felicities for the accidental equilibrium of the British Constitution. "To spare the humble and war down the proud," is a permanent idea for the policing of this planet. But that freedom should "slowly broaden down from precedent to precedent" merely happens to be the policy of the English upper class; it has no vital sanction; it might be much better to broaden quickly. One can write great poetry about a truth or even about a falsehood, but hardly about a legal fiction. The misanthropic idea, as in Byron, is not a truth, but it is one of the immortal lies. As long as humanity exists, humanity can be hated. Wherever one shall gather by himself, Byron is in the midst of him. It is a common and recurrent mood to regard man as a hopeless Yahoo. But it is not a natural mood to regard man as a hopeful Yahoo, as the Evolutionists did, as a creature changing before one's eyes from bestial to beautiful, a creature whose tail has just dropped off while he is staring at a far-off divine event. This particular compromise between contempt and hope was an accident of Tennyson's time, and, like his liberal conservatism, will probably never be found again. His weakness was not being old-fashioned or new-fashioned, but being fashionable. His feet were set on things transitory and untenable, compromises and compacts of silence. Yet he was so perfect a poet that I fancy he will still be able to stand, even upon such clouds.

The Domesticity of Detectives

I HAVE just been entertaining myself with the last sensational story by the author of *The Yellow Room*, which was probably the best detective tale of our time, except Mr. Bentley's admirable novel, *Trent's Last Case*. The name of the author of *The Yellow Room* is Gaston Leroux; I have sometimes wondered whether it is the alternative *nom de plume* of the writer called Maurice Leblanc who gives us the stories about Arsène Lupin, the gentleman burglar. There would be something very symmetrical in the inversion by which the red gentleman always writes about a detective, and the white gentleman always writes about a criminal. But I have no serious reason to suppose the red and white combination to be anything but a coincidence; and the tales are of two rather different types. Those of Gaston the Red are more strictly of the type of the mystery story, in the sense of resolving a single and central mystery. Those of Maurice the White are more properly adventure stories, in the sense of resolving a rapid succession of immediate difficulties. This is inherent in the position of the hero; the detective is always outside the event, while the criminal is inside the event. Some would express it by saying that the policeman is always outside the house when the burglar is inside the house. But there is one very French quality which both these French writers share, even when their writing is very far from their best. It is a spirit of definition which is itself not easy to define. To say it is scientific will only suggest that it is slow. It is much truer to say it is military; that is, it is something that has to be both scientific and swift. It can be seen in much greater Frenchmen, as compared with men still greater who were not Frenchmen. Jules Verne and H. G. Wells, for instance, both wrote fairy-tales of science; Mr. Wells has much the larger mind and interest in life; but he often lacks one power which Jules Verne possesses supremely—the power of going to the point. Verne is very French in his rigid relevancy; Wells is very English in his rich irrelevance. He is there as English as Dickens, the best passages in whose stories are the stoppages, and even stopgaps. In a truly French tale there are no stoppages; every word, however dull, is deliberate, or directed towards the end. The comparison could be carried further back among the classics. The romance of Dumas may seem a mere riot of swords and feathers; it is often spoken of as a mere revel in adventure and variety; the madness of romance. But it is not a mere riot, but rather a military revolution, and even a disciplined revolution; certainly, a very French revolution. It is not a mere mad revel, but a very gorgeous and elaborate banquet planned by a great cook; a very French cook. Scott was a greater man than Dumas; and a greater novelist on the note of the serious humours of humanity. But he was not so great a story-teller, because he had less of something that can only be called the strategy of the soldier. The Three Musketeers advance like an army; with their three servants and their one ally, they march, manœuvre, deploy, wheeling into positions and almost making patterns. They are always present wherever their author wants them; which is by no means true of all the characters of all the novelists. Dumas, and not Scott, ought to have written the life of Napoleon; Dumas was much nearer to Napoleon, in the fact that there was most emphatically method in his madness. Nobody ever called Scott mad; and certainly nobody could ever call him methodical. He was as incapable of the conspiracy which carried off General Monk in a box as Dumas was incapable of the curse of Meg Merrilies or the benediction of Di Vernon. But there is eternally present in the Frenchman something which may truly be called presence of mind. There to be an artist is not to be absent-minded, however harmless or happy the holidays of the mind may be. Art is to have the intellect and all its instruments on the spot and ready to go to the point; as when, but a little while ago, a great artist stood by the banks of the Marne and saved the world with one gesture of living logic—the sword-thrust of the Latin.

But though the strategy of the French story is allied to the strategy by which the French army has always affected the larger matters of mankind, I doubt whether such a story ought to deal with such matters. I mentioned at the beginning M. Gaston Leroux's last mystery story because I think I know why it is not anything like so good as his first mystery story. The truth is that there are two types of sensational romance between which our wilder sensationalists seem to waver; and I think they are generally at their strongest in dealing with the first type, and at their weakest in dealing with the second. For the sake of a convenient symbol, I may call them respectively the romance of the Yellow Room and the romance of the Yellow Peril. We might say that the great detective story deals with small things; while the small or silly detective story generally deals with great things. It deals with diabolical diplomatists darting about between Vienna and Paris and Petrograd; with vast cosmopolitan conspiracies ramifying through all the cellars of Europe; or worse and most widespread of all, occult and mystical secret societies from China or Tibet; the vast and vague Oriental terrorism which I call for convenience here the Yellow Peril. On the other hand, the good detective story is in its nature a good domestic story. It is steeped in the sentiment that an Englishman's house is his castle; even if, like other castles, it is the scene of a few quiet tortures or assassinations. In other words, it is concerned with an enclosure, a plan or problem set within certain defined limits. And that is where the French writer's first story was a model for all such writers; and where it ought to have been, but has not been a model for himself. The point about the Yellow Room is that it was a room; that is, it was a box, like the box in which Dumas kidnapped General Monk. The writer dealt with the quadrate or square which Mrs. Battle loved; the very plan of the problem looked like a problem in the Fourth Book of Euclid. He posted four men on four sides of a space and a murder was done in the middle of them; to all appearance, in spite of them; in reality, by one of them. Now a sensational novelist of the more cosmopolitan sort could, of course, have filled the story with a swarm of Chinese magicians who had the power of walking through brick walls, or of Indian mesmerists who could murder a man merely by meditating about him on the peaks of the Himalayas; or merely by so human and humdrum a trifle as a secret society of German spies which had made a labyrinth of secret tunnels under all the private houses in the world. These romantic possibilities are infinite; and because they are infinite they are really unromantic. The real romance of detection works inwards towards the household gods, even if they are household devils. One of the best of the Sherlock Holmes stories turns entirely on a trivial point of housekeeping: the provision of curry for the domestic dinner. Curry is, I believe, connected with the East; and could have been made the excuse for infinities of sham occultism and Oriental torments. The author could have brought in a million yellow cooks to poison a yellow condiment. But the author knew his business much better; and did not let what is called infinity, and should rather be called anarchy, invade the quiet seclusion of the British criminal's home. He did not let the logic of the Yellow Room be destroyed by the philosophy of the Yellow Peril. That is why I lament the fact that the ingenious French architect of the original Yellow Room seems to have made an outward step in this direction; not, indeed, towards the plains of Tibet, but towards the hardly less barbaric plains of Germany. His last book, *Rouletabille Chez Krupp*, concerns the manufacture of a torpedo big enough to smash a town; and an object of that size may be a sensation, but will not long be a secret. It may be inevitable that a French patriot should now write even his detective stories about the war; but I do not think this method will ever make the French mystery story what the war itself has been—a French masterpiece; *Gesta Dei per Francos*.

George Meredith

THE death of George Meredith was the real end of the Nineteenth Century, not that empty date that came at the close of 1899. The last bond was broken between us and the pride and peace of the Victorian age. Our fathers were all dead. We were suddenly orphans: we all felt strangely and sadly young. A cold, enormous dawn opened in front of us; we had to go on to tasks which our fathers, fine as they were, did not know, and our first sensation was that of cold and undefended youth. Swinburne was the penultimate, Meredith the ultimate end.

It is not a phrase to call him the last of the Victorians: he really is the last. No doubt this final phrase has been used about each of the great Victorians one after another from Matthew Arnold and Browning to Swinburne and Meredith. No doubt the public has grown a little tired of the positively last appearance of the Nineteenth Century. But the end of George Meredith really was the end of that great epoch. No great man now alive has its peculiar powers or its peculiar limits. Like all great epochs, like all great things, it is not easy to define. We can see it, touch it, smell it, eat it; but we cannot state it. It was a time when faith was firm without being definite. It was a time when we saw the necessity of reform without once seeing the possibility of revolution. It was a sort of exquisite interlude in the intellectual disputes: a beautiful, accidental truce in the eternal war of mankind. Things could mix in a mellow atmosphere. Its great men were so religious that they could do without a religion. They were so hopefully and happily republican that they could do without a republic. They are all dead and deified; and it is well with them. But we cannot get back into that well-poised pantheism and liberalism. We cannot be content to be merely broad: for us the dilemma sharpens and the ways divide.

Of the men left alive there are many who can be admired beyond expression; but none who can be admired in this way. The name of that powerful writer, Mr. Thomas Hardy, was often mentioned in company with that of Meredith; but the coupling of the two names is a philosophical and chronological mistake. Mr. Hardy is wholly of our own generation, which is a very unpleasant thing to be. He is shrill and not mellow. He does not worship the unknown God: he knows the God (or thinks he knows the God), and dislikes Him. He is not a pantheist: he is a pandiabolist. The great agnostics of the Victorian age said there was no purpose in Nature. Mr. Hardy is a mystic; he says there is an evil purpose. All this is as far as possible from the plenitude and rational optimism of Meredith. And when we have disposed of Mr. Hardy, what other name is there that can even pretend to recall the heroic Victorian age? The Roman curse lies upon Meredith like a blessing: "Ultimus suorum moriatur"—he has died the last of his own.

The greatness of George Meredith exhibits the same paradox or difficulty as the greatness of Browning; the fact that simplicity was the centre, while the utmost luxuriance and complexity was the expression. He was as human as Shakespeare, and also as affected as Shakespeare. It may generally be remarked (I do not know the cause of it) that the men who have an odd or mad point of view express it in plain or bald language. The men who have a genial and everyday point of view express it in ornate and complicated language. Swinburne and Thomas Hardy talk almost in words of one syllable; but the philosophical upshot can be expressed in the most famous of all words of one syllable—damn. Their words are common words; but their view (thank God) is not a common view. They denounce in the style of a spelling-book; while people like Meredith are unpopular through the very richness of their popular sympathies. Men like Browning or like Francis Thompson praise God in such a way sometimes that God alone could possibly understand the praise. But they mean all men to understand it: they wish every beast and fish and flying thing to take part in the applauding chorus of the cosmos. On the other hand, those who have bad news to tell are much more explicit, and the poets whose object it is to depress the people take care that they do it. I will not write any more about those poets, because I do not profess to be impartial or even to be good-tempered on the subject. To my thinking, the oppression of the people is a terrible sin; but the depression of the people is a far worse one.

But the glory of George Meredith is that he combined subtlety with primal energy: he criticized life without losing his appetite for it. In him alone, being a man of the world did not mean being a man disgusted with the world. As a rule, there is no difference between the critic and ascetic except that the ascetic sorrows with a hope and the critic without a hope. But George Meredith loved straightness even when he praised it crookedly: he adored innocence even when he analysed it tortuously: he cared only for unconsciousness, even when he was unduly conscious of it. He was never so good as he was about virgins and schoolboys. In one curious poem, containing many fine lines, he actually rebukes people for being quaint or eccentric, and rebukes them quaintly and eccentrically. He says of Nature, the great earth-mother, whom he worshipped:

> ... She by one sure sign can read,
> Have they but held her laws and nature dear;
> They mouth no sentence of inverted wit.
> More prizes she her beasts than this high breed
> Wry in the shape she wastes her milk to rear.

That is the mark of the truly great man: that he sees the common man afar off, and worships him. The great man tries to be ordinary, and becomes extraordinary in the process. But the small man tries to be mysterious, and becomes lucid in an awful sense—for we can all see through him.

The Irishman

THE other day I went to see the Irish plays, recently acted by real Irishmen—peasants and poor folk—under the inspiration of Lady Gregory and Mr. W. B. Yeats. Over and above the excellence of the acting and the abstract merit of the plays (both of which were considerable), there emerged the strange and ironic interest which has been the source of so much fun and sin and sorrow—the interest of the Irishman in England. Since we have sinned by creating the Stage Irishman, it is fitting enough that we should all be rebuked by Irishmen on the stage. We have all seen some obvious Englishman performing a Paddy. It was, perhaps, a just punishment to see an obvious Paddy performing the comic and contemptible part of an English gentleman. I have now seen both, and I can lay my hand on my heart (though my knowledge of physiology is shaky about its position) and declare that the Irish English gentleman was an even more abject and crawling figure than the English Irish servant. The Comic Irishman in the English plays was at least given credit for a kind of chaotic courage. The Comic Englishman in the Irish plays was represented not only as a fool, but as a nervous fool; a fussy and spasmodic prig, who could not be loved either for strength or weakness. But all this only illustrates the fundamental fact that both the national views are wrong; both the versions are perversions. The rollicking Irishman and the priggish Englishman are alike the mere myths generated by a misunderstanding. It would be rather nearer the truth if we spoke of the rollicking Englishman and the priggish Irishman. But even that would be wrong too.

Unless people are near in soul they had better not be near in neighbourhood. The Bible tells us to love our neighbours, and also to love our enemies; probably because they are generally the same people. And there is a real human reason for this. You think of a remote man merely as a man; that is, you think of him in the right way. Suppose I say to you suddenly—"Oblige me by brooding on the soul of the man who lives at 351 High Street, Islington." Perhaps (now I come to think of it) you *are* the man who lives at 351 High Street, Islington. In that case substitute some other unknown address and pursue the intellectual sport. Now you will probably be broadly right about the man in

Islington whom you have never seen or heard of, because you will begin at the right end—the human end. The man in Islington is at least a man. The soul of the man in Islington is certainly a soul. He also has been bewildered and broadened by youth; he also has been tortured and intoxicated by love; he also is sublimely doubtful about death. You can think about the soul of that nameless man who is a mere number in Islington High Street. But you do not think about the soul of your next-door neighbour. He is not a man; he is an environment. He is the barking of a dog; he is the noise of a pianola; he is a dispute about a party wall; he is drains that are worse than yours, or roses that are better than yours. Now, all these are the wrong ends of a man; and a man, like many other things in this world, such as a cat-o'-nine-tails, has a large number of wrong ends, and only one right one. These adjuncts are all tails, so to speak. A dog is a sort of curly tail to a man; a substitute for that which man so tragically lost at an early stage of evolution. And though I would rather myself go about trailing a dog behind me than tugging a pianola or towing a rose-garden, yet this is a matter of taste, and they are all alike appendages or things dependent upon man. But besides his twenty tails, every man really has a head, a centre of identity, a soul. And the head of a man is even harder to find than the head of a Skye terrier, for man has nine hundred and ninety-nine wrong ends instead of one. It is no question of getting hold of the sow by the right ear; it is a question of getting hold of the hedgehog by the right quill, of the bird by the right feather, of the forest by the right leaf. If we have never known the forest we shall know at least that it is a forest, a thing grown grandly out of the earth; we shall realize the roots toiling in the terrestrial darkness, the trunks reared in the sylvan twilight.

But to find the forest is to find the fringe of the forest. To approach it from without is to see its mere accidental outline ragged against the sky. It is to come close enough to be superficial. The remote man, therefore, may stand for manhood; for the glory of birth or the dignity of death. But it is difficult to get Mr. Brown next door (with whom you have quarrelled about the creepers) to stand for these things in any satisfactorily symbolic attitude. You do not feel the glory of his birth; you are more likely to hint heatedly at its ingloriousness. You do not, on purple and silver evenings, dwell on the dignity and quietude of his death; you think of it, if at all, rather as sudden. And the same is true of historical separation and proximity. I look forward to the same death as a Chinaman; barring one or two Chinese tortures, perhaps. I look back to the same babyhood as an ancient Phœnician; unless, indeed, it were one of that special Confirmation class of Sunday-school babies who were passed through the fire to Moloch. But these distant or antique terrors seem merely tied on to the life: they are not part of its texture. Babylonian mothers (however they yielded to etiquette) probably loved their children; and Chinamen unquestionably reverenced their dead. It is far different when two peoples are close enough to each other to mistake all the acts and gestures of everyday life. It is far different when the Baptist baker in Islington thinks of Irish infancy, passed amid Popish priests and impossible fairies. It is far different when the tramp from Tipperary thinks of Irish death, coming often in dying hamlets, in distant colonies, in English prisons or on English gibbets. There childhood and death have lost all their reconciling qualities; the very details of them do not unite, but divide. Hence England and Ireland see the facts of each other without guessing the meaning of the facts. For instance, we may see the fact that an Irish housewife is careless. But we fancy falsely that this is because she is scatter-brained; whereas it is, on the contrary, because she is concentrated—on religion, or conspiracy, or tea. You may call her inefficient, but you certainly must not call her weak. In the same way, the Irish see the fact that the Englishman is unsociable; they do not see the reason, which is that he is romantic.

This seems to me the real value of such striking national sketches as those by Lady Gregory and Mr. Synge, which I saw last week. Here is a case where mere accidental realism, the thing written on the spot, the "slice of life," may, for once in a way, do some good. All the signals, all the flags, all the declaratory externals of Ireland we are almost certain to mistake. If the Irishman speaks to us, we are sure to misunderstand him. But if we hear the Irishman talking to himself, it may begin to dawn on us that he is a man.

Ireland and the Domestic Drama

In a sense so gigantic that it would have staggered the statesman who once used the phrase, we have called in the new world to redress the balance of the old. The new world has found new worlds to conquer; it has new tasks not only drastic but delicate, not only political but psychological. Among the things which America may yet help us to achieve is one about which I feel strongly and even painfully—the reconciliation, a thousand times thwarted but now a thousand times more necessary, between the English and the Irish. The triangular table of such a peace conference need not, and perhaps had better not, be found in any public building. Rather it should be found in every public house and even in every private house. The change should come through something which is far nobler and more eternal than diplomacy or politics; talk. It should come through the only real public opinion, which is always uttered in private; the public opinion that is a mass of private opinions. A famous Irishman said of the Irish that they were too poetical to be poets, but that they were the greatest talkers since the Greeks. My personal memory does not stretch back to the greatest period of Greece; and perhaps the best talker I ever knew was an Irishman, who is now living in America and (I will confidently affirm) talking in America. It may be true that he is too poetical to be a poet; anyhow, he is not too poetical to be the father of a poet. He is Mr. J. B. Yeats, the father of Mr. W. B. Yeats; and he has lately been persuaded to write and print some of the good things he has said all his life—first in the form of a book of letters, and later of a book of essays, *Essays Irish and American*, published by Mr. Fisher Unwin. But my real satisfaction, in the social and political sense, is to know not that he has written a little, but that he has spoken much; for out of such seemingly lost and wasted words come the real international understandings.

There was a type of detachment during the late war, not to be confused with what I can only call the view of the vulgar peacemonger. It was not the patronizing pacifism of the gentleman who took a holiday in the Alps and said he was "above the struggle"; as if there were any Alp from which the soul can look down on Calvary. There is, indeed, one mountain among them that might be very appropriate to so detached an observer—the mountain named after Pilate, the man who washed his hands. The isolation I mean is far removed from such impudence. The defence of this detachment is that it is not really detached; it was not indifference, but indignation. It was not without foundation; it was only without proportion. Indeed, the real case against it was that while its expression was largely cynical, its motive was largely sentimental. Such was the irritation of Mr. Bernard Shaw; such was the irritation of many Irishmen much more national than Mr. Bernard Shaw. Their irritation can be analysed in a simple phrase; it annoyed them that the men who were wrong should be right. It annoyed them that all the snobs and sneaks of our corrupt parliamentarianism should free the world by accident. In the quarrel with Prussia, they could not really doubt—they did not really doubt—that England was right. But they did doubt whether England had any right to be right.

It is a view I think self-stultifying and even suicidal. For the great work will be remembered and the meaner workers forgotten; and it is madness to praise the Persians on the eve of Marathon because one has quarrelled with some silly archon at Athens, whose very name will be lost in a few years. But it is not a treasonable, far less a treacherous view; and its anger is the same as the popular anger it arouses. This is the Irish mood which common sense and common sympathy must deal with; and this is the peculiar value of real Irish intellectual detachment like that of Mr. Yeats. First of all, a man like Mr. Yeats is so genuinely detached that he can be definite and clear in his sympathy with the Allies. He would be capable of the supreme impartiality of seeing that England could be right although she had been wrong; and even that Ireland could be wrong although she had been wronged. But all the time he would play with a perennial fount of satire and insight on the fundamental spiritual facts that falsify the English position in Ireland. He would make us feel that we were only right in one thing because we were so wrong in many things. There are many examples of this in his little book of essays; but the one I would emphasize here especially is his very vital point about the domestic nature of the whole sociology of Ireland. Here again he is all the more impressive for being in a sense impartial, or even what some would call indifferent. He is not what is called orthodox; he might well be called sceptical. He has cultivated rather Continental æsthetics than Catholic apologetics. It is solely by a serene insight into what his French teachers would call the *vraie verité* that he sees the way the world ought to go; and pauses upon the phrase, "the return to the home."

Irish education, he declares, must always depend on the fact that the child's mind is full of "the drama of the home." It marks his judicial emancipation that he contrasts this domestic drama favourably with two other types of teaching, one of which would be called conventional and conservative, while the other would be called unconventional and advanced. He criticizes the old English public-school boy; he also criticizes (I grieve to state) the new American woman. The two things called in England the "public school" and the "high school" are counted almost contraries, merely because one is old and the other new. But the critic sees them to be essentially the same; because in both cases the school overshadows the home. Here is a profound practical instance of the root realities of the Irish national claim. Here is a case in which Home Rule literally means the rule of the home. It will never be possible to establish the English fashion in Ireland, and I for one should not pretend to be sorry if it were possible to spread the Irish fashion to England.

For the drama of the home is really very dramatic. It is one of those facts that are confused and hidden by the modern fuss about social machinery, which is the mere scene-shifting and stage-carpentering of the domestic drama. The household is the lighted stage, on which the actors appeal literally to the gods. It is in private life that things happen. A human being is born at home; he generally dies at home, and the social philosophy that can deal with nothing but his coffin carried out of the house is merely a philosophy of boxes and parcels, a philosophy of luggage and labels. Half our human effort is now wasted on mere transit, transport, and exchange; the commonwealth is a clearing-house of cases we never open and presents we never enjoy. Rulers and reformers are a race of rather pedantic porters, always carrying an unknown present to an unknown person, not unfrequently (I fancy) the wrong present to the wrong person.

Some of our strenuous social organizers may be content to spend Christmas at Charing Cross Station for the pride of controlling the traffic and the luggage. But I confess I find it more exciting to be at the end of the journey where the Christmas gifts can be seen.

The Japanese

Is it not time that we western people protested against being perpetually browbeaten with the high morality of the Orient—especially of Japan? I remember a curious occasion some years ago when certain able journalists on a Socialist paper in Fleet Street suddenly burst into a blazing excitement about King Asoka. Their relations with this prince could not be called intimate; in point of fact, he died some thousands of years ago somewhere in the middle of Asia. But it seemed that in him we had lost our only reliable moral guide. Religion was a failure, and human life, on the whole, a tragedy; but King Asoka was all right. He was faultlessly just, infinitely merciful, the mirror of the virtues, the prop of the poor. Outsiders were naturally interested in the sources of this revelation. And after some discussion it was discovered and mildly pointed out that this description of the King's virtues is only found on a few of the King's own official inscriptions. Old Asoka may have been a very nice man, but we have only his own word for it that he was so nice as all that. And even in the benighted West it might not be impossible to find monarchs who were very just and mighty according to their own proclamations; and courts that were quite exemplary in the *Court Circular*. It had never struck these simple Asokites in Fleet Street that the pompous enunciation of ideals probably meant no more in Bengal than in Birmingham, in the ancient East than in the modern West. It is as if a Hindoo should say that under the sublime French monarchy every King had to be a good Christian; for he was called on coins and parchments "the most Christian King." It is as if an Arab said that honour was so high and sensitive among English M.P.'s that they constantly called each other, with a burst of admiration, "The Honourable Member for Tooting." It could hardly be more absurd if the Japanese declared that an English Duke must have an elegant figure, for they had seen an allusion to "His Grace." And yet it is with just this comic solemnity that we are asked to accept the moral pretensions of the East to-day, and especially the moral pretensions of Japan. My eye has just fallen upon two newspaper paragraphs, each of which exclaimed mournfully what a pity it was that we had not the high conception of chivalric devotion which the Japanese call

"Bushido," or some such name. As if we had no chivalrous principles in Europe! And as if they had no unchivalrous practices in the Far East! If we see no beauty in Excalibur, are we likely to take more seriously the two swords of some outlandish Daimio? If we are truly dumb after the death of Roland, are we likely to shout with enthusiasm at the sight of a *hara-kiri*?

Here is, perhaps, the queerest case of all. Many of these Orientalists have lately been filled with horror at finding that Young Turks still propose to be Turkish, and that advanced Japan is still unaccountably Japanese. Dr. Parker damned Abdul Hamid. These modern humanitarians cannot understand any people wishing to get rid of Abdul Hamid without also wishing to become exactly like Dr. Parker. In the same way they are horrified that the Japanese Government has very abruptly condemned some criminals said to be conspiring against the sacred person of the Mikado. It never seems to occur to them that you can take off a Turk's turban without taking off his head; and that, under a Brixton bowler, the head would go on thinking the same thoughts. It never seems to strike them that the man of the Far East still has a yellow skin, even when you have also given him a yellow press. But the most astounding version of the thing I found in the following paragraph, the opening paragraph of an article on the Japanese condemnations in an influential weekly paper:

"Japan has followed Western ways in a great many respects, but it is saddening to learn that she is adopting the most reprehensible methods of Russia and Spain in dealing with men and women who have the intelligence to be ahead of their time and have the courage to avow their opinions."

This really strikes me as colossal. I quite agree that Japan has imitated many Western things; I also think that Japan has mostly imitated the worst Western things. That is the cause of my very defective sympathy with Japan. If the Japanese had imitated Dante or mediæval architecture, if they had imitated Michelangelo or Italian painting, if they had imitated Rousseau and the French Revolution—then I, as a European, should have felt at least flattered. But the Japanese have only imitated the worst things of our worst period: the inhuman commercialism of Birmingham; the inhuman militarism of Berlin. I feel as if I had looked in a mirror and seen a monkey. Or, if this metaphor be counted uncharitable, I feel just as some coarse but kindly man might feel if a little brother began to imitate only his vices. I say this to show how easily I embrace the idea that Japan might borrow from us bad things as well as good; and then I turn with astonishment—nay, consternation—to the paragraph I have quoted. Japan (it seems) has borrowed from Russia and Spain the reprehensible habit of executing people without adequate trial. Trial by jury, with complete reports in the newspapers next day, was the common practice all over the Far East until the dreadful example of Spain somehow crept across two continents and destroyed it. Such a thing as autocratic execution was unknown in the East. Such a notion as that of despotism had never occurred to the Japanese. Up to that last lost moment when they heard of Russia, County Councils had been buzzing in every town, republics established in every island of the East. Before the European came, polling-booths were at the end of every street and ballot-boxes rattled over all Asia. But, alas! they heard of Spain. They heard that in Spain the trials of rebels in arms had occasionally been conducted in secret; and this was enough to destroy the long and famous tradition of free democracy in the Far East.

Now I do think that, compared with this amazing bosh, Gilbert's *Mikado*, with his punishment "lingering, with boiling oil in it," might be called a good, solid, sensible picture of Japan. Eastern despotism has many advantages; and I do not doubt that many of its decisions were not "lingering," but as rough and rapid as they were just. But to what mental state have people come if they cannot see that Europe has been, upon the whole, the home of democracy, and Asia, upon the whole, the home of despotism? Really, Japan is not so barren of resource as this writer supposes. The Far East really has no need to go to Russia for autocracy, or to Spain for torture. It has done very artistic things in that way itself. And if Spain and Russia have indeed terrorized and tortured, it is much more historically likely that they got it from Asia than that Asia ever had the slightest need to borrow it from them.

The plain facts, of course, are perfectly simple. Japan has borrowed our guns and telephones, but she has not borrowed our morality; and, morally speaking, I really do not see why she should. Under all Japan's elaborate armour-plating she is still the same strange, heathen, sinister, and heroic thing: she has still the two deep Oriental habits, prostration before despotism and ferocity of punishment. She still thinks, in the Eastern style, that a king is infinitely sublime: the brother of the sun and moon. She still thinks, in the Eastern style, that a criminal is infinitely punishable; "something with boiling oil in it." Why on earth should Japan abandon the adoration of the Mikado and the destruction of his enemies, merely because a scientific apparatus has made the Mikado more victorious and the destruction of his enemies more easy?

Christian Science

I HAVE read recently, within a short period of each other, two books that stand in an odd relation, and illustrate the two ways of dealing with the same truth. The first was Mrs. Eddy's *Science and Health,* and the other a very interesting collection of medical and ecclesiastical opinion called *Medicine and the Church.* It is edited by Mr. Geoffrey Rhodes, and published by Kegan Paul. Of the first work, the Christian Science Bible, my recollections are somewhat wild and whirling. My most vivid impression is of one appalling passage to the effect that the continued perusal of this book through the crisis of an illness had always been followed by recovery. The idea of reading any book "through the crisis of an illness" is rather alarming. But I incline to agree that anyone who could read *Science and Health* through the crisis of an illness must be made of an adamant which no malady could dissolve. Nevertheless, it is a mistake to oppose Christian Science on the impossibility or even the improbability of its cures. There is always this tendency for normal men to attack abnormalities on the wrong ground; their arguments are as wrong as their antagonism is right. Thus the only sensible argument against Female Suffrage is that, with her social and domestic powers, woman is as strong as man. But silly people will attack Female Suffrage on the ground that she is weaker than man. Or, again, the only sensible argument against Socialism is that every man ought to have private property. But the wretched Anti-Socialists will give themselves away by trying to maintain that only a few people ought to have property, and even that only in the shape of monstrous American trusts. In the same way, there is great danger that the modern world may give battle to Mrs. Eddy upon the wrong *terrain,* and give her the opportunity (or, rather, her more clear-headed lieutenants) of claiming some popular success. There is such a thing as spiritual healing. No one has ever doubted it except one dingy generation of materialists in chimney-pot hats. If we seem to stand with the materialists, and Mrs. Eddy seems to stand for the healing, she will have a chance of success. A man whose toothache has left off will think with gratitude of the healer, and with some indifference of the scientist explaining the difference between functional and organic toothaches. I will grant what Mrs. Eddy does to people's bodies. It is what she does to their souls that I object to.

Mrs. Eddy summarizes the substance of her creed in the characteristic sentence: "But in order to enter into the kingdom, the anchor of Hope must be cast beyond the veil of matter into the Shekinah into which Jesus has passed before us." Now personally I should prefer to sow the anchor of Hope in the furrows of primeval earth; or to fill the anchor to the brim with the wine of human passion; or to urge the anchor of hope to a gallop with the spurs of moral energy; or simply to pluck the anchor, petal by petal, or spell it out letter by letter. But whatever slightly entangled metaphor we take to express our meaning, the essential difference between Mrs. Eddy's creed and mine is that she anchors in the air, while I put an anchor where the groping race of men have generally put it, in the ground. And this very fact, that we have always thought of hope under so rooted and realistic a figure, is a good working example of how the popular religious sense of mankind has always flowed in the opposite direction to Christian Science. It has flowed from spirit to flesh, and not from flesh to spirit. Hope has not been thought of as something light and fanciful, but as something wrought in iron and fixed in rock.

In short, the first and last blunder of Christian Science is that it is a religion claiming to be purely spiritual. Now, being purely spiritual is opposed to the very essence of religion. All religions, high and low, true and false, have always had one enemy, which is the purely spiritual. Faith-healing has existed from the beginning of the world; but faith-healing without a material act or sacrament—never. It may be the ancient priest, curing with holy water, or the modern doctor curing with coloured water. In either case you cannot do without the water. It may be the upper religion with its bread and wine, or the under religion with its eye of newt and toe of frog: in both cases what is essential is the right materials. Savages may invoke their demons over the dying, but they do something else as well. To do them justice, they dance round the dying, or yell, or do something with their bodies. The Quakers (I mean the really admirable, old-fashioned Quakers) were far more ritualistic than any Ritualists. The only difference between a Ritualist curate and a Quaker was that the Quaker wore his queer vestments all the time. The Peculiar People do without doctors; but they do not do without oil. They are not so peculiar as all that.

The book which Mr. Geoffrey Rhodes has edited is just what was wanted for the fixing of these facts of flesh and spirit. When I was a boy, people used to talk about something which they called the quarrel between religion and science. It would be very tedious to recount the quarrel now; the rough upshot of it was something like this: that some traditions too old to be traced came in vague conflict with some theories much too new to be tested. Many things three thousand years old had forgotten their reason for existing; many things a few years old had not yet discovered theirs. To this day this remains roughly true of all the relations between science and religion. The truths of religion are unprovable; the facts of science are unproved.

It really looks just now as if a reconciliation would be made between religion and science, a reconciliation well embodied in Mr. Rhodes's work. I will not any longer dispute the divine mission of Mrs. Eddy. I think she was supernaturally sent on earth to reconcile all the parsons and all the doctors in a healthy hatred of herself. Here *is* the reconciliation of science and religion; you will find it in *Medicine and the Church*. In this interesting book all the clerics become as medical as they can, and all the doctors become as clerical as they can, with the one honourable object of keeping out the healer. The chaplain sits on one side of the bed and the physician on the other, while the healer hovers around, baffled and furious. And they do well; for there really is a great link between them. It is the link of the union of flesh and spirit, which the heresy of the healer blasphemes. The priest may have taken his spirit with a little flesh, or the doctor his flesh with a little spirit; but the union was essential to both. With the religious there might be much prayer and a little oil; with the scientific there might be much oil (castor oil) and precious little prayer. But no religion disowned sacraments and no doctors disowned sympathy. And they are right to combine together against the great and horrible heresy—the horrible heresy that there can be such a thing as a purely spiritual religion.

The Lawlessness of Lawyers

JUDGE Parry is one of the men who have done mountains of good merely by being alive; while many judges act as if they were already dead, not to say ... but Judge Parry might misunderstand a misuse of theological imagery. He is somewhat anti-clerical; which seems a waste of talent in a country where there is no clericalism. In his last book, *Law and the Woman*, I find much with which I do not agree, yet nothing which is not agreeable. Not only does he say everything with a disarming humour and candour; but even in error he never loses sight of the large fact: that sex relations do not depend on the exceptional action of law, but on the normal action of creed and custom. Alone among such lawyers he understands that the poor live on laughter as on a fairy-tale; and can be more scientifically studied in the fictions of Jacobs than the facts of Webb. I might pursue the view further than he on some points; as when he would infer the mere enslavement of women from some stories about the selling of wives. He is doubtless correct in detail; but the rhyme he gives to prove his point may almost be said to disprove it. He quotes a jolly ballad about a man who tried to sell his wife with a halter round her neck and, failing to do so, tried to hang himself in the halter rather than go on living with her. Obviously this is simply the fable of the grey mare; and does not mean that the man ruled his wife, but rather that she ruled him. I do not agree about divorce; but I am not going to argue about it here, or about any such problem of the sexes. This is partly because I should have to begin about the nature of a vow, and it feels like talking to a judge about the nature of an oath, and might almost be contempt of court. But it is more, I hope, for the manlier reason that I do want to argue about something else.

I think this delightful book might really mislead by a view of progress which over-simplifies history: the view that "the thoughts of men are widened by the process of the suns"—a monotonous process which cannot even widen itself. He begins his story of the subjection of women from the Bible story of Adam and Eve. He then proceeds at once to quote, not the Bible, but John Milton, and says it is almost exactly in the form "in which mediæval man was wont to explain to mediæval woman the kind of thing she really was." Now whatever Milton was, he was not mediæval. He was, in his own opinion and in real though relative truth, highly modern and rationalistic. And he would have regarded his somewhat contemptuous view of woman as part of his emancipation from mediævalism. Probably the very same attitude made him approve of divorce; and makes the difference between woman's place in his epic and her place in Dante's. On either side of that Gothic gateway of the Middle Ages out of which he had emerged (as he would have said) into the daylight, there had stood two symbolic statues of women, at least of equal importance in the scheme. One represented the weak woman by whom Satan had entered the world; the other the strong woman by whom God had entered the world. Milton and his Puritans deliberately battered and obliterated the image of the good woman and carefully preserved the bad woman, to be a standing reproach to womanhood. But they unquestionably thought their anti-feminist iconoclasm was a great step in progress; and the fact illustrates what an uncommonly crooked and even backward path the path called progress has really been. Nor is it difficult to discover, even in the writer's own account, whence this anti-feminism iconoclasm drew its force; which was certainly not merely from the Book of Genesis. Judge Parry says, perhaps disputably, that the rude Saxons had more legal regard for women than the Romans. But assuming for the sake of argument that the heathen Romans did give a low status to woman, they clearly cannot have got it either from the Hebrew Scriptures or the mediæval Church. If he will ask where they did get it, he will probably also find where Milton got it. The truth is that there was an element of intellectual brutality in the Renaissance and revival of the pagan world. The very worship of power and reason embodied itself in a preference for the sex that was supposed superior in them. New tyrannies as well as new liberties were encouraged by the New Learning; and Cervantes was laughing at the unreal adventurer who fancied he was unchaining captives, at the very time when Hawkins, the real adventurer, was first leading negroes in chains.

Those chains may be linked up again presently in the chain of my own argument: here I use the matter merely to show the danger of trusting each ethical fashion as it comes. There is one matter on which I would respectfully and seriously differ from Judge Parry; and that does not concern laws about women, but rather law itself. In praising the judgment in the Jackson Case, despite its technical irregularity, he speaks of a fine example of our judge-made law, and says: "But that is one of the sane and healthy attributes of our judicial system. There comes a breaking-point where a great judge recognizes that the precedents in the books are obsolete, and what has to be stated is the justice of the case according to the now existing standard of human righteousness." Now it is surely as plain as a pikestaff that this doctrine makes a small number of very wealthy old gentlemen in wigs absolute despots over the whole commonwealth. The Emperor of China was supposed to state the justice of the case. The Sultan of the Indies was supposed to judge by the existing standard of human righteousness. If the judges are not restrained by the law, what are they restrained by, which every autocrat on earth has not claimed to be restrained by?

Now there is certainly a case for personal and arbitrary government; and as there are good sultans, so there are good judges. I should not be afraid to appear before Judge Parry (if I may presume to imagine myself innocent) though he were surrounded with janissaries in a secret divan, or delivering dooms under an oak tree in a wild, prehistoric forest. I should not mind his having the power to skin me or boil me in oil; for I feel sure he would "recognize that these precedents were obsolete" and not do it. But it is by no means true that the confidence I should feel in Judge Parry would be extended to any judge who talked about obsolete precedents and human righteousness. Quite the contrary, if anything. I trust him because he often takes the side of the under-dog. I should not trust a man who always took the side of the opinion which happened to be top-dog. He understood, for instance, the case for "Pro-Boers"; but in the mafficking time a dozen great judges would have strained any law to make a case against Pro-Boers. Feminism was the fashion and may have produced some acts of justice; but Imperialism was also the fashion and might have produced any acts of any injustice. There is, let us suppose, an old statute that certain prisoners may be tortured for evidence; but the judges disregard it, and Judge Parry is satisfied. But there are three very vital reasons why he should not be satisfied. First, it encourages legislators to be lazy and leave a bad statute they ought to repeal. Second, they leave it so that it can be resharpened in some reaction or panic against particular people, who *will* be tortured. And third, and most important of all, the same judge who has said that prisoners must not be tortured for evidence may say some fine morning that prisoners may be vivisected for scientific inquiry; and he may have the same reason for saying the one as the other, the simple reason that such talk is fashionable in his set. And the set is very small and very rich; we are dealing strictly with fashion and not even, in any large sense, with public opinion. The standards of that world are often special and sometimes rather secretive. Judge Parry even quotes a "paradox" of Lord Reading to the effect that persons like himself should administer justice and not law. Law is narrow and national, and might possibly lead a British Minister to look no further than the British Parliament as an appropriate place for telling the truth. But justice, being international and surveying the world from China to Peru, perceives without difficulty the office of the one particular Parisian newspaper which has the right to insist on an explanation.

But the vital point is this. Judge Parry gives the instance of a judgment in which Mansfield, overriding certain remote precedents and quaint survivals, declared that there cannot be slaves in England. I am sorry to mention such a detail, but the fact is that the same judge made law is now declaring in the same way that there *can* be slaves in England. A magistrate has forbidden men to leave an employer, though the contract had admittedly terminated. Practical courts are overriding the obsolete and remote precedent of some man, far in the mists of mediævalism, who is said to have made a free contract with a wealthier fellow-creature. They are disregarding the quaint survivals in our language, whereby the hand holding the tool is described as "his" hand. Our more vivid modern speech calls the man himself a hand; merely one of the many hands of his Briarean master. "There comes a breaking-point"; and it is liberty that is broken.

Whether the silent millions approve this judgment, or the other judgments, liberal or servile, feminist or anti-feminist, which Judge Parry quotes, I will not debate, but I leave the query to his very fair consideration. For if those silent millions spoke, I fancy they would surprise us in many matters, but most of all in the discovery of how little they think of all of us, judges, lawyers, literary fellows, and the rest. But I am very certain that Judge Parry would be found among the few, among the very few, who amid all the insolence of our inconsistencies have never lost that rare and even awful thing, the respect of the poor.

Our Latin Relations

IT is odd how often one may hear, in the middle of a very old and genuine English town, the remark, that it looks like a foreign town. I heard it only yesterday, standing on the ramparts of the noble hill of Rye, which overlooks the flats like a Mount of St. Michael left inland. Most people know that Rye contains a mediæval monument which might almost be called a mediæval prophecy—a prophecy of modern things more awful than anything mediæval. It is an ancient tower, which has not only always been marked on maps with the name of Ypres, but has always been actually pronounced by the name of Wipers. Nothing could mark a thing as more continuously national than that Englishmen sundered by vast centuries should actually make the same mistake and should mispronounce the same word in the same way.

There is in this small point a paradox we must understand, especially just now, if we are to have a really patriotic foreign policy. It is very unlucky that for some time our teaching of history has been rather the unteaching of history, because it has been the unteaching of tradition. Our histories told us we were Teuton; our legends told us we were Roman—and, as usual, the legends were right. It is not only true that England is nowhere more really English than where she is Roman—it is even true that she is nowhere more really English than where she is French. To take only the chance example, with which I began above, you could find nothing more national, more typical, more traditional, as a real piece of English history, than the very phrase "The Cinq Ports." And it is all the more English because the word "cinq" is French and the word "port" is Latin. A Teutonist professor, full of some folly about "folk-speech," might insist on our calling them "The Five Harbours," or (for all I know) "The Five Holes." But his version would be less popular, and only more pedantic. The Latin was always the popular element, which may not sound so odd if we happen to remember that the very word "popular" is Latin.

Thus our alliance with the French and the Italians is not something to be supported for the sake of the last five years. It is something to be solidified for the sake of more than a thousand. The fact has been hidden by the historical accident that we have often been the antagonists of the French in particular rivalries for particular things. But we were always much nearer to the French when we were their antagonists than to the Germans when we were their Allies. There was much more resemblance between a knight like the Black Prince and a knight like Bertrand du Guesclin than there ever was between a sailor like Nelson and a soldier like Blücher. A town like Rye is full of memories of fighting with the French, especially in the Middle Ages; of raids to and fro across the narrow seas, in which the bells of the coast-town churches were captured and recaptured; and there are spirited stories about the Abbot of Battle, worthy to be turned into ballads. But the very fact of these coast-town raids suggests that it was coast against coast, and even seaman against seaman. But the whole point of Prussian war was that it was an inland thing; the whole point of English war that it was an island thing. The alliance with Prussia was never either popular or natural; it was wholly aristocratic and artificial. Compared with that, the mediæval war was as friendly as a mediæval tournament. Nor was it peculiar to the case of France; it was true of all we call Latin—all that remains of the Roman Empire. The Latins, even when treated as foes in politics, were treated almost as friends in popular tradition. The English sailors sang in their idle moments "Farewell and adieu to you, fine Spanish ladies," even when they had devoted their working hours to singeing the beards of the fine Spanish gentlemen. The children in the nurseries sang in imaginative triumph "The King of Spain's daughter came to visit me," though their Elizabethan parents might have been lighting the beacons and calling out the train-bands to prevent the King of Spain's son, the noble Don John of Austria, from paying them such a visit. A thousand nursery rhymes and nonsense tags testify to a vast popular tradition that Southern Europe was the world to which we belonged. We belonged to a system of which Rome was the sun, and of which the old Roman provinces were planets. We were never meant to pursue a meteor out of empty space, the comet of Teutonism. Our place was in an order and a watch of stars, though one star might differ from another in glory. Our place was with that red star of Gaul which might well bear the name of Mars; or that morning and evening star which the Latins themselves named Lucifer, last to fade and first to return in every twilight of history; Italy, the light of the world.

A Latin alliance is founded on our history, though not on our historians. The French and English who fought each other round these southern harbours were also ready to help each other, and often did help each other. Not only did they frequently go crusading together against the Turks, but they would have been ready at any moment to go crusading against the Prussians. Chaucer was exceedingly English, and therefore partly French; and he sends his ideal knight to fight the heathen in Prussia. Froissart was highly French, and therefore respectful to the English; and he says that the French and English always do courtesy, but the Germans never. The truth is that all the old English traditions, scholarly and legendary, chivalric and vulgar, were at one in referring back to Roman culture, until we come to a new crop of very crude pedants in the nineteenth century.

Most of them were prigs, and many of them were snobs—for it was largely a Court fashion, spread by Court poets and Court chaplains. It was like a huge, hideous, gilded German monument; and, fortunately, it has already fallen down. But I think it undesirable that the mere discredited litter and lumber of it, left lying about, should for ever prevent us from building anything else.

Even after the ghastly enlightenment of the war there are people who cannot clear their minds of the notion that the Prussian is the Progressive. They think he is progressing now, because he is picking up new things. Picking up new things is not the way to progress, any more than picking up grass by the roots is the way to make it grow. The northern barbarian always has picked up new things, especially when they were other people's things. It was still only picking up new things, whether it was picking pockets or picking brains. And there was always one other note about the new things—that they never lived to be old. The barbarians followed the creed of Arius as they followed the ensign of Attila. But nobody remembers Attila as everybody remembered Alfred; and, though some modern people object to hearing the Athanasian Creed, they have no opportunity of objecting to hearing the Arian Creed. The enthusiasms of semi-savages do not last.

On Pigs as Pets

A DREAM of my pure and aspiring boyhood has been realized in the following paragraph, which I quote exactly as it stands:

A complaint by the Epping Rural District Council against a spinster keeping a pig in her house has evoked the following reply: "I received your letter, and felt very much cut up, as I am laying in the pig's room. I have not been able to stand up or get on my legs; when I can, I will get him in his own room, that was built for him. As to getting him off the premises, I shall do no such thing, as he is no nuisance to anyone. We have had to be in the pig's room now for three years. I am not going to get rid of my pet. We must all live together. I will move him as soon as God gives me strength to do so."

The Rev. T. C. Spurgin observed: "The lady will require a good deal of strength to move her pet, which weighs forty stone."

It appears to me that the Rev. T. C. Spurgin ought, as a matter of chivalry, to assist the lady to move the pig, if it is indeed too heavy for her strength; no gentleman should permit a lady, who is already very much cut up, to lift forty stone of still animated and recalcitrant pork; he should himself escort the animal downstairs. It is an unusual situation, I admit. In the normal life of humanity the gentleman gives his arm to the lady, and not to the pig; and it is the pig who is very much cut up. But the situation seems to be exceptional in every way. It is all very well for the lady to say that the pig is no nuisance to anyone: as it seems that she has established herself in the pig's private suite of apartments, the question rather is whether she is a nuisance to the pig. But indeed I do not think that this poor woman's fad is an inch more fantastic than many such oddities indulged in by rich and reputable people; and, as I say, I have from my boyhood entertained the dream. I never could imagine why pigs should not be kept as pets. To begin with, pigs are very beautiful animals. Those who think otherwise are those who do not look at anything with their own eyes, but only through other people's eyeglasses. The actual lines of a pig (I mean of a really fat pig) are among the loveliest and most luxuriant in nature; the pig has the same great curves, swift and yet heavy, which we see in rushing water or in rolling cloud. Compared to him, the horse, for instance, is a bony, angular, and abrupt animal. I remember that Mr. H. G. Wells, in arguing for the relativity of things (a subject over which even the Greek philosophers went to sleep until Christianity woke them up), pointed out that, while a horse is commonly beautiful if seen in profile, he is excessively ugly if seen from the top of a dogcart, having a long, lean neck, and a body like a fiddle. Now, there is no point of view from which a really corpulent pig is not full of sumptuous and satisfying curves. You can look down on a pig from the top of the most unnaturally lofty dogcart; you can (if not pressed for time) allow the pig to draw the dogcart; and I suppose a dogcart has as much to do with pigs as it has with dogs. You can examine the pig from the top of an omnibus, from the top of the Monument, from a balloon, or an airship; and as long as he is visible he will be beautiful. In short, he has that fuller, subtler, and more universal kind of shapeliness which the unthinking (gazing at pigs and distinguished journalists) mistake for a mere absence of shape. For fatness itself is a valuable quality. While it creates admiration in the onlookers, it creates modesty in the possessor. If there is anything on which I differ from the monastic institutions of the past, it is that they sometimes sought to achieve humility by means of emaciation. It may be that the thin monks were holy, but I am sure it was the fat monks who were humble. Falstaff said that to be fat is not to be hated; but it certainly is to be laughed at, and that is a more wholesome experience for the soul of man.

I do not urge that it is effective upon the soul of a pig, who, indeed, seems somewhat indifferent to public opinion on this point. Nor do I mean that mere fatness is the only beauty of the pig. The beauty of the best pigs lies in a certain sleepy perfection of contour which links them especially to the smooth strength of our south English land in which they live. There are two other things in which one can see this perfect and piggish quality: one is in the silent and smooth swell of the Sussex downs, so enormous and yet so innocent. The other is in the sleek, strong limbs of those beech trees that grow so thick in their valleys. These three holy symbols, the pig, the beech tree, and the chalk down, stand for ever as expressing the one thing that England as England has to say—that power is not inconsistent with kindness. Tears of regret come into my eyes when I remember that three lions or leopards, or whatever they are, sprawl in a fantastic, foreign way across the arms of England. We ought to have three pigs passant, gardant, or on gules. It breaks my heart to think that four commonplace lions are couched around the base of the Nelson Column. There ought to be four colossal Hampshire hogs to keep watch over so national a spot. Perhaps some of our sculptors will attack the conception; perhaps the lady's pig, which weighs forty stone and seems to be something of a domestic problem, might begin to earn its living as an artist's model.

Again, we do not know what fascinating variations might happen in the pig if once the pig were a pet. The dog has been domesticated—that is, destroyed. Nobody now in London can form the faintest idea of what a dog would look like. You know a Dachshund in the street; you know a St. Bernard in the street. But if you saw a Dog in the street you would run from him screaming. For hundreds, if not thousands, of years no one has looked at the horrible hairy original thing called Dog. Why, then, should we be hopeless about the substantial and satisfying thing called Pig? Types of Pig may also be differentiated; delicate shades of Pig may also be produced. A monstrous pig as big as a pony may perambulate the streets like a St. Bernard without attracting attention. An elegant and unnaturally attenuated pig may have all the appearance of a greyhound. There may be little, frisky, fighting pigs like Irish or Scotch terriers; there may be little pathetic pigs like King Charles spaniels. Artificial breeding might reproduce the awful original pig, tusks and all, the terror of the forests—something bigger, more mysterious, and more bloody than the bloodhound. Those interested in hairdressing might amuse themselves by arranging the bristles like those of a poodle. Those fascinated by the Celtic mystery of the Western Highlands might see if they could train the bristles to be a veil or curtain for the eye, like those of a Skye terrier; that sensitive and invisible Celtic spirit. With elaborate training one might have a sheep-pig instead of a sheep-dog, a lap-pig instead of a lap-dog.

What is it that makes you look so incredulous? Why do you still feel slightly superior to the poor lady who would not be parted from her pig? Why do you not at once take the hog to your heart? Reason suggests his evident beauty. Evolution suggests his probable improvement. Is it, perhaps, some instinct, some tradition ...? Well, apply that to women, children, animals, and we will argue again.

The Romance of Rostand

ROSTAND, the romantic dramatist of France, and a very national poet, died almost on the day of the great national triumph. He had lived, to use his own imaginative heraldry, to see the golden eagles of Gaul and Rome drive back the black eagles of Prussia and Austria. He was too much of an earlier generation to take the precise part of Pequy or Claudel in the process which banished the birds of barbaric night from the land of the Eagles of the sun. But the part he had played in that earlier time might well merit the use of a kindred metaphor, drawn from his own fairyland of ornithology. He had a special claim to use as one of his titles the noble mediæval name of Chantecler. He might well be called the Gallic cock in that earlier twilight of vultures and bats. The end of the nineteenth century was a time of pessimism for Europe, and especially of pessimism for France; for pessimism was the shadow of Prussianism. Rostand was really a cock that crowed before the coming of sunrise. When it came it was red as blood; but the sun rose.

But that mediæval nickname of the cock contains a still more appropriate criticism. The word "clear" is always a clue to Rostand's country, and to Rostand's work. He suffered in the decadent days, he suffers to some extent still, from a strange blunder which supposes that what is clear must be shallow. It is chiefly founded on false figures of speech; and is akin to the mysteriously meaningless saying that still waters run deep. It is repeated without the least reference to the evident fact that the stillest of all waters do not run at all. They lie about in puddles, which are none the less shallow because they are covered with scum. Such were the North German philosophies fashionable at the end of the nineteenth century; men believed in the puddle's profundity solely because of its opacity. When the decadent critics sneered at Rostand's popularity, they were simply sneering at his lucidity. They were protesting against his power of conveying what he meant in the most direct and telling fashion. They were complaining bitterly because he did not think with a German accent, which is nearly the same thing as an impediment in the speech. The wit with which all his dialogues blazed was also a positive disadvantage in that muddle-headed modern world, which even now will only begin to realize gradually the greatness of France. Nothing has been so senselessly underrated as wit, even when it seems to be the mere wit of words. It is dismissed as merely verbal; but, in fact, it is more solemn writing that is merely verbal, or rather merely verbose. A joke is always a thought; it is grave and formal writing that can be quite literally thoughtless. This applies to jokes when they are not only quite verbal but quite vulgar. A good pun, or even a bad pun, is more intellectual than mere polysyllables. The man, the presumably prehistoric man, who invented the phrase, "When is a door not a door; when it's ajar," made a serious and successful mental effort of selection and combination. But a Prussian professor might begin on the same problem, "When is a door not a door; when its doorishness is a becoming rather than a being, and when the relativity of doorishness is co-ordinated with the evolution of doors from windows and skylights, of which approximation to new function, etc. etc."—and the Prussian professor might go on like that for ever, and never come to the end because he would never come to the point. A pun or a riddle can never be in that sense a fraud. Real wisdom may be better than real wit, but there is much more sham wisdom than there is sham wit.

This is the immediate point about Rostand, who had very real wit, but wit of a very poetic and sometimes epic order. It is very characteristic of him, and very puzzling to his critics, that he was witty even in repudiating wit. In the scene of *Cyrano de Bergerac*, in which the hero pleads in his friend's name against the preciosity of the heroine, he quite naturally uses the phrase touching the evaporation of truth in artificial terminology, "Et que le fin du fin ne soit la fin des fins." That involves a pun and also involves a point; and it is a subject on which it would be quite easy to be earnest and pointless. A philosopher need never come to an end in talking about ends; precisely because he is not required to amuse anybody, he is not really required to mean anything. Every page, every paragraph, almost every line of Rostand's plays bristles with these points, which are both verbal and vital. If any critic thinks it was easy to produce them by the hundred, there is an exceedingly easy test; let him try to produce one. In attempting to joke in this fashion, he will probably find himself thinking for the first time. For that matter, merely to make one of the better puns of *Punch* or *Hood's Annual* would be enough to stump most of the sceptics who have been taught in the Teutonic schools to think a thing creative because it is chaotic, and vast because it is vague. A modern "thinker" will find it easier to make up a hundred problems than to make up one riddle. For in the case of the riddle he has to make up the answer.

The drama of Rostand was full of answers, if they seem to the superficial merely to be ringing repartees. In the ballade of the duel the hero says that the sword-thrust shall come at the end of the envoi, but something like it seems to come continually at the end of the line. But these retorts are really much more than superficial, because they have the ring of dogma, of affirmation and certainty, and therefore of triumph. The wit is heroic wit; and his sub-title was strictly correct when he called *Cyrano* a heroic comedy. It was written in a literary period which was far too pessimistic to rise even to heroic Tragedy. It will grow in value in a more virile time, when the air has been cleared by a great crusade. Rostand's poetry will certainly remain. It may not remain among the very greatest poetry, for the very reason that he fulfilled the office rather of the trumpet than the lyre. But he himself may well have shared the spirited taste of his own hero, and have preferred that something even more noble than the laurel should remain as a feather in his cap.

Wishes

MOST of us, I suppose, have amused ourselves with the old and flippant fancy of what poets or orators would feel like if their wild wishes came true. The poet would be not a little surprised if the (somewhat inadequate) wings of a dove suddenly sprouted from his shoulder-blades. And I suspect that even the baby who cries for the moon would be rather frightened if it fell out of the sky, crushing forests and cities like a colossal snowball, shutting out the stars and darkening the earth it had illuminated. Shelley was magnificently moved when he wished to be a cloud driven before the wild West Wind: but even Shelley would have been not a little disconcerted if he had found himself turning head-over-heels in mid-air the instant he had written the line. He would even be somewhat relieved, I fancy, to fall upon the thorns of life and bleed a little more. When Keats, the human nightingale, lay listening to the feathered one, he expressed a strong desire for a long drink of red wine. In this I believe him to have accurately analysed his own sentiments. But when he proceeds to explain that he is strongly inclined at that moment to wish himself dead, I entertain strong doubts as to whether he is equally exact, and am by no means certain that he would really like "to cease upon the midnight" even "with no pain." Such sceptical fantasies, I say, have occurred to most of us; they do not spoil fine poetry for those who really like it; they only salt it with humour and human fellowship. Things seriously beautiful are, perhaps, the only things that we can jest about with complete spiritual safety. One cannot insult the poem except by being afraid of the parody.

But I think there is another and more curious cause for this common human fancy of a wild wish which is disappointed by being fulfilled. The idea is very common, of course, in popular tradition: in the tale of King Midas; in the tale of the Black Pudding; in the tale of the Goloshes of Fortune. My own personal feeling about it, I think, is that a world in which all one's wishes were fulfilled would, quite apart from disappointments, be an unpleasant world to live in. The world would be too like a dream, and the dream too like a nightmare. The Ego would be too big for the Cosmos; it would be a bore to be so important as that. I believe a great part of such poetic pleasure as I have comes from a certain disdainful indifference in actual things. Demeter withered up the cornfields: I like the cornfields because they grow in spite of me. At least, I can lay my hand on my heart and say that no cornfield ever grew with my assistance. Ajax defied the lightning; but I like the lightning because it defies me. I enjoy stars and the sun or trees and the sea, because they exist in spite of me; and I believe the sentiment to be at the root of all that real kind of romance which makes life not a delusion of the night, but an adventure of the morning. It is, indeed, in the clash of circumstances that men are most alive. When we break a lance with an opponent the whole romance is in the fact that the lance does break. It breaks because it is real: it does not vanish like an elfin spear. And even when there is an element of the marvellous or impossible in true poetry, there is always also this element of resistance, of actuality and shock. The most really poetical impossibility is an irresistible force colliding with an immovable post. When that happens it will be the end of the world.

It is true, of course, that marvels, even marvels of transformation, illustrate the noblest histories and traditions. But we should notice a rather curious difference which the instinct of popular legend has in almost all cases kept. The wonder-working done by good people, saints and friends of man, is almost always represented in the form of restoring things or people to their proper shapes. St. Nicholas, the Patron Saint of Children, finds a boiling pot in which two children have been reduced to a sort of Irish stew. He restores them miraculously to life; because they ought to be children and ought not to be Irish stew. But he does not turn them into angels; and I can remember no case in hagiology of such an official promotion. If a woman were blind, the good wonder-workers would give her back her eyes; if a man were halt, they would give him back his leg. But they did not, I think, say to the man: "You are so good that you really ought to be a woman"; or to the woman: "You are so bothered it is time you had a holiday as a man." I do not say there are no exceptions; but this is the general tone of the tales about good magic. But, on the other hand, the popular tales about bad magic are specially full of the idea that evil alters and destroys the personality. The black witch turns a child into a cat or a dog; the bad magician keeps the Prince captive in the form of a parrot, or the Princess in the form of a hind; in the gardens of the evil spirits human beings are frozen into statues or tied to the earth as trees. In all such instinctive literature the denial of identity is the very signature of Satan. In that sense it is true that the true God is the God of things as they are—or, at least, as they were meant to be. And I think that something of this healthy fear of losing self through the supernatural is behind the widespread sentiment of the Three Wishes; the sentiment which says, in the words of Thackeray:

Fairy roses, fairy rings
Turn out sometimes troublesome things.

Now the transition may seem queer; but this power of seeing that a tree is *there*, in spite of you and me, that it holds of God and its own treeishness, is of great importance just now in practical politics. We are in sharp collision with a large number of things, some of which are real facts and all of which are real faiths. We must see these things objectively, as we do a tree; and understand that they exist whether we like them or not. We must not try and turn them into something different by the mere exercise of our own minds, as if we were witches. I happen to think, for instance, that it is silly of Orangemen to think they would be persecuted under Home Rule. But I think it is sillier to think that the Orangemen do not think so. It is sillier not to see that a man can fire off a gun for a prejudice as well as he can for an ideal. I disagree with the Orangemen; I don't disagree with the Nationalists; but I deny neither. I sympathize with the Labour revolt; I don't sympathize with the Feminist revolt; but I deny neither. Then, again, both these latter tendencies have succeeded in colliding violently with another reality, the priests of the ancient popular creed of Ireland. They achieved that catastrophe, not because they did not believe the creed, but because they could not even believe that it was believed.

Now you can, if you choose, pass your life in a wizard dream, in which all your enemies are turned into something else. You can insist that a priest is only a parrot, or a Suffragette always a wandering hind: but if you do, you will sooner or later get into your head what is meant by an immovable post.

The Futurists

THERE are still people talking about Futurism, though I should have thought it was now a thing of the past, exploded by its own silly gunpowder train of progressive theory. If a man only believed the world was round because his grandmother said it was flat, another man had only to say it was spiral in order to be a more advanced idiot than either of them. But, after all, the world is one shape and not another (I don't care which myself, but certainly one), and will be when we all die, and would have been if no worm or weed had ever lived. And it amuses me to notice that the very Agnostics who still quote Galileo's phrase about the earth, "And yet it moves!" are the very people who talk as if truth could be different from age to age—as if the whole world was a different shape when you or I were in a different frame of mind. Progressives of this kind *cannot* say "And yet it moves" save in the sense that their own foot can roll it about like a football, or that their own finger can stop it as Joshua's stopped the moon. They may control Nature like witches; but they cannot appeal to Nature like Galileo. They have no abiding objective fact to which to appeal. On the mere progressive theory there is no more immortality about the astronomy of Galileo than the medicine of Galen.

But one or two interesting ideas can be found in Futurist speculations, essays, lectures, books, etc.—indeed, the Futurists can be interesting everywhere but in their pictures. And this is the difficulty of all such movements—the lack of the final fulfilment. I will not put it offensively, as by saying that they write a beautiful prospectus, but there are no funds. I do not mean it like that. I will put it poetically by saying that there are beautiful leaves and flowers, but there is no fruit. There are leaves of learning enough to fill a library; there are flowers of rhetoric enough to last a session. They are all about a picture: and there is no picture. Thus Mr. Nevinson, the eminent English Futurist, has explained that pictorial art should be as independent of natural facts as music is: it should not imitate, but utter. Of music, of course, the remark is true, and fairly familiar. Certainly three notes on a piano can bring tears to the eyes by reminding us of a dead friend: though certainly the first noise is not the noise he made when whistling to his dog, nor the second the noise he made when kicking his boots off, nor the third the noise he made when blowing his nose. Perhaps the three notes are noises he could never have made: perhaps he was unmusical, like many magnificent people—I am unmusical myself. Perhaps, I say, he was unmusical: yet music can express him. This is an interesting fact; but it is only one fact, and the examination of a few others would have shown Mr. Nevinson the shallowness of his artistic philosophy.

But Mr. Nevinson and the Futurists, having never seen a fact before in their lives, clutch hold of this one and rush after the car of progress like poor baby-laden charwomen after a motorbus. Their deduction is this: As his favourite song recalls the friend, though it contains none of his grunts, snorts, or sneezes, so his portrait would better recall his appearance if it contained no trace of his eyes, nose, mouth, hair (if any), masculine sex, anthropoid or erect posture, or any other oddity by which his friends were in the habit of distinguishing him from a lamp-post or a large whale, or from the works of Creation in general. Mr. Nevinson says that the most pungent and passionate emotions (such, presumably, as we have about friendship and even about love) can be conveyed by planes, mathematical proportions, arbitrary or abstract colours, arrangements of line, and all the things we most of us instinctively associate with carpets, if not with oilcloth. "It is possible," he says. It is. It is not a contradiction in terms. But if I say, "It is possible by arranging a tomato, ten pearl buttons, a copy of the second and last number of a Tariff Reform weekly, one wooden leg, three odd boots, and a bag with a hole in it, to induce your worst enemy to burst into tears and give you a million pounds in conscience money," then, if you are a Monist and a fool, you will answer that it could not happen. But if you are an Agnostic and a Christian, you will answer that you tried it on with your worst creditor, and it didn't work with him. Nor would the planes, angles, abstract colours work with him. They don't work with you; they don't work with me; they don't work with anybody. And the reason simply is that these philosophers, like so many modern philosophers, do not possess the patience to see what they are taking for granted. Have you ever seen a fellow fail at the high jump because he had not gone far enough back for his run? That is Modern Thought. It is so confident of where it is going to that it does not know where it comes from.

The quite simple fallacy is this. The only thing we know about the things we call the Arts is that when they are good they all stir the soul in a somewhat similar way. Their roots in savagery or civilization are so different and so dark, their relations to utility or practical life are so prodigiously contrasted, the mere time or space they occupy is so unequal in every case, the psychological explanations of their very existence are so inconsistent and anarchic, that we simply do not know whether in one single point we can argue from one art to another. We do not know enough about it, and there is an end of the matter. For instance, many have compared classic poetry with classic architecture; and anyone who has ever felt the virginity and dignity of either will know what such a comparison means. Milton spoke of "building" a line of poetry; and nobody seems able to talk about sonnets without talking about marble. But in technical fact the analogy is only a fancy, after all. Treat it for one moment as Mr. Nevinson treats the analogy between music and painting, and it is pure, preposterous nonsense—like Futurism.

Who will deny that height, or the appearance of height, is one of the effects of architecture? Who has not read or said or felt that some wall seemed too enormous for any mortals to have made, that some domes seemed to occupy heaven, or that some spire seemed to strike him out of the sky? But who, on the other hand, ever said that his sonnet was printed higher up on the page than somebody else's sonnet? Who ever either praised or disliked a piece of verse according to its vertical longitude? Who ever said, "My sonnet occupied five volumes of the *Times*, but you *should* see it pasted all in one piece"? Who ever said, "I have written the tallest triolet on earth"?

Mr. Nevinson will bring a tear to my eye by exhibiting a pattern and calling it a picture on the same day when he induces me to read two hundred leading articles in the *Times* simply by calling them a tower. They have many of the qualities of a tower: they are long; they are symmetrical; they are all built out of the same old bricks; they sometimes stand upright, like the Tower of Giotto; they more often lean very much, like the Tower of Pisa; they most frequently fall down altogether, and fall on the wrong people, like the Tower of Siloam. One could pursue such abstract fancies for ever, but the simple fact remains—and it is a fact of the senses. The thing is not a tower, because it does not tower. And the Futurist picture is not a picture, because it does not depict. Why one art can do without shapes, and another without words, and another without movement, and another without massiveness, and why each of these is necessary to one or other of them separately—all this we shall know when we know what art means. And I cannot say that the Futurists have helped us much in finding out.

The Evolution of Emma

AMONG the many good critical tributes to the genius of Jane Austen, to the fine distinction of her humour, the sympathetic intimacy of her satire, the easy exactitude of her unpretentious style, which have appeared in celebration of her centenary, there is one criticism that is naturally recurrent: the remark that she was quite untouched by the towering politics of her time. This is intrinsically true; nevertheless it may easily be used to imply the reverse of the truth. It is true that Jane Austen did not attempt to teach any history or politics; but it is not true that we cannot learn any history or politics from Jane Austen. Any work so piercingly intelligent of its own kind, and especially any work of so wise and humane a kind, is sure to tell us much more than shallower studies covering a larger surface. I will not say much of the mere formality of some of the conventions and conversational forms; for in such things it is not only not certain that change is important, but it is not even certain that it is final. The view that a thing is old-fashioned is itself a fashion; and may soon be an old fashion. We have seen this in many recurrences of female dress; but it has a deeper basis in human nature. The truth is that a phrase can be falsified by use without being false in fact; it can seem stale without being really stilted. Those who see a word as merely worn out, fail to look forward as well as back. I know of two poems by two Irish poets of two different centuries, essentially on the same theme; the lover declaring that his love will outlast the mere popularity of the beauty. One is by Mr. Yeats and begins: "Though you are in your shining days." The other is by Tom Moore and begins: "Believe me, if all those endearing young charms." The latter language strikes us as ridiculously florid and over-ripe; but Moore was far from being ridiculous. Believe me (as he would say), it was no poetaster who wrote those hackneyed words about the silent harp and the heart that breaks for liberty. And if English were read some day by strangers as a classic language, I am not sure that "endearing" would not endure as a better word than "shining"; or even that (after some repetition and reaction) it might not seem as strained to say "shining" as to say "shiny." Yet Mr. Yeats also is a great poet, as I called him last week; only the printer or somebody altered it to a "good" one—a mysteriously moderate emendation. Similarly, when one of Jane Austen's heroines wants to say that the hero is a good fellow, she expresses confidence in what she calls "his worth." This goads her younger modern readers to madness; yet in truth the term is far more philosophic and eternal than the terms they would use themselves. They would probably say he was "nice," and Jane Austen would indeed be avenged. For the best of her heroes, Henry Tilney, himself foresaw and fulminated against the unmeaning ubiquity of that word, a prophet of the pure reason of his age, seeing in a vision of the future the fall of the human mind.

Negatively, of course, the historic lesson from Jane Austen is enormous. She is perhaps most typical of her time in being supremely irreligious. Her very virtues glitter with the cold sunlight of the great secular epoch between mediæval and modern mysticism. In that small masterpiece, *Northanger Abbey*, her unconsciousness of history is itself a piece of history. For Catherine Morland was right, as young and romantic people often are. A real crime *had* been committed in Northanger Abbey. It is implied in the very name of Northanger Abbey. It was the crucial crime of the sixteenth century, when all the institutions of the poor were savagely seized to be the private possessions of the rich. It is strange that the name remains; it is stranger still that it remains unrealized. We should think it odd to go to tea at a man's house and find it was still called a church. We should be surprised if a gentleman's shooting box at Claybury were referred to as Claybury Cathedral. But the irony of the eighteenth century is that Catherine was healthily interested in crimes and yet never found the real crime; and that she never really thought of it as an abbey, even when she thought of it most as an antiquity.

But there is a positive as well as a negative way in which her greatness, like Shakespeare's, illuminates history and politics, because it illuminates everything. She understood every intricacy of the upper middle class and the minor gentry, which were to make so much of the mental life of the nineteenth and twentieth centuries. It is said that she ignored the poor and disregarded their opinions. She did, but not more than all our Governments and all our Acts of Parliaments have done. And at least she did consistently ignore them; she ignored where she was ignorant. Well it would have been for the world if others had ignored the working-class until they understood it as well as she did the middle class. She was not a student of sociology; she did not study the poor. But she did study the students—or at least the social types which were to become the students of the poor. She knew her own class, and knew it without illusions; and there is much light on later problems to be found in her delicate delineation of vanities and snobberies and patronage. She had to do with the human heart; and it is that which cometh out of the heart that defileth a nation, philanthropy, efficiency, organization, social reform. And if the weaker brethren still wonder why we should find in Baby Week or Welfare Work a dangerous spirit, from which its best adherents find it hard to free themselves, if they doubt how such a danger can be reconciled with the personal delicacy and idealism of many of the women who work such things, if they think that fine words or even fine feelings will guarantee a respect for the personality of the poor, I really do not know that they could do better than sit down, I trust not for the first time, to the reading of *Emma*.

For all this that has happened since might well be called the Evolution of Emma. That unique and formidable institution, the English Lady, has, indeed, become much more of a public institution; that is, she has made the same mistakes on a much larger scale. The softer fastidiousness and finer pride of the more gracious eighteenth-century heroine may seem to make her a shadow by comparison. It seems cruel to say that the breaking off of Harriet's humbler engagement foreshadows the indiscriminate development of Divorce for the Poor. It seems horrible to say that Emma's small matchmaking has in it the seed of the pestilence of Eugenics. But it is true. With a gentleness and justice and sympathy with good intentions, which clear her from the charge of common cynicism, the great novelist does find the spring of her heroine's errors, and of many of ours. That spring is a philanthropy, and even a generosity, secretly founded on gentility. Emma Woodhouse was a wit, she was a good woman, she was an individual with a right to her own opinion; but it was because she was a lady that she acted as she did, and thought she had a right to act as she did. She is the type in fiction of a whole race of English ladies, in fact, for whom refinement is religion. Her claim to oversee and order the social things about her consisted in being refined; she would not have admitted that being rich had anything to do with it; but as a fact it had everything to do with it. If she had been very much richer, if she had had one of the great modern fortunes, if she had had the wider modern opportunities (for the rich) she would have thought it her duty to act on the wider modern scale; she would have had public spirit and political grasp. She would have dealt with a thousand Robert Martins and a thousand Harriet Smiths, and made the same muddle about all of them. That is what we mean about things like Baby Week—and if there had been a baby in the story, Miss Woodhouse would certainly have seen all its educational needs with a brilliant clearness. And we do not mean that the work is done entirely by Mrs. Pardiggle; we mean that much of it is done by Miss Woodhouse. But it is done because she *is* Miss Woodhouse and not Martha Muggins or Jemina Jones; because the Lady Bountiful is a lady first, and will bestow every bounty but freedom.

It is noted that there are few traces of the French Revolution in Miss Austen's novels; but, indeed, there have been few traces of it in Miss Austen's country. The peculiarity which has produced the situation I describe is really this: that the new sentiment of humanitarianism has come, when the old sentiment of aristocracy has not gone. Social superiors have not really lost any old privileges; they have gained new privileges, including that of being superior in philosophy and philanthropy as well as in riches and refinement. No revolution has shaken their secret security or menaced them with the awful peril of becoming no more than men. Therefore their social reform is but their social refinement grown restless. And in this old teacup comedy can be found, far more clearly appreciated than in more ambitious books about problems and politics, the psychology of this mere restlessness in the rich, when it first stirred upon its cushions. Jane Austen described a narrow class, but so truthfully that she has much to teach about its after adventures, when it remained narrow as a class and broadened only as a sect.

The Pseudo-Scientific Books

THERE is a certain kind of modern book which must, if possible, be destroyed. It ought to be blown to pieces with the dynamite of some great satirist like Swift or Dickens. As it is, it must be patiently hacked into pieces even by some plodding person like myself. I will do it, as George Washington said, with my little hatchet; though it might take a long time to do it properly. The kind of book I mean is the pseudo-scientific book. And by this I do not mean that the man who writes it is a conscious quack or that he knows nothing; I mean that he proves nothing; he simply gives you all his cocksure, and yet shaky, modern opinions and calls it science. Books are coming out with so-called scientific conclusions—books in which there is actually no scientific argument at all. They simply affirm all the notions that happen to be fashionable in loose "intellectual" clubs, and call them the conclusions of research. But I am no more awed by the flying fashions among prigs than I am by the flying fashions among snobs. Snobs say they have the right kind of hat; prigs say they have the right kind of head. But in both cases I should like some evidence beyond their own habit of staring at themselves in the glass. Suppose I were to write about the current fashions in dress something like this: "Our ignorant and superstitious ancestors had straight hat-brims; but the advance of reason and equality has taught us to have curly hat-brims; in early times shirt-fronts are triangular, but science has shown that they ought to be round; barbaric peoples had loose trousers, but enlightened and humane peoples have tight trousers," and so on, and so on. You would naturally rebel at this simple style of argument. You would say—"But, hang it all, give us some facts. Prove that the new fashions are more enlightened. Prove that men think better in the new hats. Prove that men run faster in the new trousers."

I have just read a book which has been widely recommended, which is introduced to the public by Dr. Saleeby, and which is, I understand, written by a Swiss scientist of great distinction. It is called *Sexual Ethics*, by Professor Forel. I began to read the book, therefore, with respect. I finished reading it with stupefaction. The Swiss Professor is obviously an honest man, though too Puritanical to my taste, and I am told that he does really know an enormous lot about insects. But as for the conception of proving a case, as for any notion that a "new" opinion needs proof, and that it is not enough, when you knock down great institutions, to say that you don't like them—it is clear that no such conceptions have ever crossed his mind. Science says that man has no conscience. Science says that man and woman must have the same political powers. Science says that sterile unions are morally free and without rule. Science says that it is wrong to drink fermented liquor. And all this with a splendid indifference to the two facts—first, that "Science" does not say these things at all, for numbers of great scientists say exactly the opposite; and second, that if Science did say these things, a person reading a book of rationalistic ethics might be permitted to ask why. Professor Forel may have mountains of evidence which he has no space to exhibit. We will give him the benefit of that doubt, and pass on to points where any thinking man is capable of judging him.

Where this sort of scientific writer is seen in all his glory is in his first abstract arguments about the nature of morality. He is immense; he is at once simple and monstrous, like a whale. He always has one dim principle or prejudice: to prove that there is nothing separate or sacred about the moral sense. Professor Forel holds this prejudice with all possible decorum and propriety. He always trots out three arguments to prove it; like three old broken-kneed elephants. Professor Forel duly trots them out. They are supposed to show that there is no such thing positively existing as the conscience; and they might just as easily be used to show that there are no such things as wings or whiskers, or toes or teeth, or boots or books, or Swiss Professors.

The first argument is that man has no conscience because some men are quite mad, and therefore not particularly conscientious. The second argument is that man has no conscience because some men are more conscientious than others. And the third is that man has no conscience because conscientious men in different countries and quite different circumstances often do very different things. Professor Forel applies these arguments eloquently to the question of human consciences; and I really cannot see why I should not apply them to the question of human noses. Man has no nose because now and then a man has no nose—I believe that Sir William Davenant, the poet, had none. Man has no nose because some noses are longer than others or can smell better than others. Man has no nose because not only are noses of different shapes, but (oh, piercing sword of scepticism!) some men use their noses and find the smell of incense nice, while some use their noses and find it nasty. Science therefore declares that man is normally noseless; and will take this for granted for the next four or five hundred pages, and will treat all the alleged noses of history as the quaint legends of a credulous age.

I do not mention these views because they are original, but exactly because they are not. They are only dangerous in Professor Forel's book because they can be found in a thousand books of our epoch. This writer solemnly asserts that Kant's idea of an ultimate conscience is a fable because Mohammedans think it wrong to drink wine, while English officers think it right. Really he might just as well say that the instinct of self-preservation is a fable because some people avoid brandy in order to live long, and some people drink brandy in order to save their lives. Does Professor Forel believe that Kant, or anybody else, thought that our consciences gave us direct commands about the details of diet or social etiquette? Did Kant maintain that, when we had reached a certain stage of dinner, a supernatural voice whispered in our ear "Asparagus"; or that the marriage between almonds and raisins was a marriage that was made in heaven? Surely it is plain enough that all these social duties are deduced from primary moral duties—and may be deduced wrong. Conscience does not suggest "asparagus," but it does suggest amiability, and it is thought by some to be an amiable act to accept asparagus when it is offered to you. Conscience does not respect fish and sherry; but it does respect any innocent ritual that will make men feel alike. Conscience does not tell you not to drink your hock after your port. But it does tell you not to commit suicide; and your mere naturalistic reason tells you that the first act may easily approximate to the second.

Christians encourage wine as something which will benefit men. Teetotallers discourage wine as something that will destroy men. Their conscientious conclusions are different, but their consciences are just the same. Teetotallers say that wine is bad because they think it moral to say what they think. Christians will not say that wine is bad because they think it immoral to say what they don't think. And a triangle is a three-sided figure. And a dog is a four-legged animal. And Queen Anne is dead. We have, indeed, come back to alphabetical truths. But Professor Forel has not yet even come to them. He goes on laboriously repeating that there cannot be a fixed moral sense, because some people drink wine and some people don't. I cannot imagine how it was that he forgot to mention that France and England cannot have the same moral sense, because Frenchmen drive cabs on the right side of the road and Englishmen on the left.

The Humour of King Herod

IF I say that I have just been very much amused with a Nativity play of the fourteenth century it is still possible that I may be misunderstood. What is more important, some thousand years of very heroic history will be misunderstood too. It was one of the Coventry cycle of mediæval plays, loosely called the Coventry Mysteries, similar to the Chester Mysteries and the Towneley Mysteries.

And I was not amused at the blasphemy of something badly done, but at a buffoonery uncommonly well done. But, as I said at the time, the educated seem to be very ignorant of this fine mediæval fun. When I mentioned the Coventry Mystery many ladies and gentlemen thought it was a murder in the police news. At the best, they supposed it to be the title of a detective story. Even upon a hint of history they could only recall the story of Godiva; which might be called rather a revelation than a mystery.

Now I always read police news and I sometimes write detective stories; nor am I at all ashamed of doing either. But I think the popular art of the past was perhaps a little more cheerful than that of the present. And in seeing this Bethlehem drama I felt that good news might perhaps be as dramatic as bad news; and that it was possibly as thrilling to hear that a child is born as to hear that a man is murdered.

Doubtless there are some sentimental people who like these old plays merely because they are old. My own sentiment could be more truly stated by saying that I like them because they are new. They are new in the imaginative sense, making us feel as if the first star were leading us to the first child.

But they are also new in the historical sense, to most people, owing to that break in our history which makes the Elizabethans seem not merely to have discovered the new world but invented the old one. Nobody could see this mediæval play without realizing that the Elizabethan was rather the end than the beginning of a tradition; the crown and not the cradle of the drama.

Many things that modern critics call peculiarly Elizabethan are in fact peculiarly mediæval. For instance, that the same stage could be the place where meet the extremes of tragedy and comedy, or rather farce. That daring mixture is always made a point of contrast between the Shakespearean play and the Greek play or the French classical play. But it is a point of similarity, or rather identity, between the Shakespearean play and the miracle play.

Nothing could be more bitterly tragic than the scene in this Nativity drama, in which the mothers sing a lullaby to the children they think they have brought into safety the moment before the soldiers of Herod rush in and butcher them screaming on the stage. Nothing could be more broadly farcical than the scene in which King Herod himself pretends that he has manufactured the thunderstorm.

In one sense, indeed, the old religious play was far bolder in its burlesque than the more modern play. Shakespeare did not express the unrest of King Claudius by making him fall over his own cloak. He did not convey his disdain for tyranny by letting Macbeth appear with his crown on one side. This was partly no doubt an improvement in dramatic art; but it was partly also, I think, a weakening of democratic satire.

Shakespeare's clowns are philosophers, geniuses, demigods; but Shakespeare's clowns are clowns. Shakespeare's kings may be usurpers, murderers, monsters; but Shakespeare's kings are kings. But in this old devotional drama the king is the clown. He is treated not so much with disdain as with derision; not so much with a bitter smile as with a broad grin. A cat may not only look at a king but laugh at a king; like the mythical Cheshire cat, an ancient cat as terrible as a tiger and grinning like a gargoyle. But that Cheshire cat has presumably vanished with the Chester Mysteries, the counterpart of these Coventry Mysteries; it has vanished with the age and art of gargoyles.

In other words, that popular simplicity that could see wrongful power as something pantomimically absurd, a thing for practical jokes, has since been sophisticated by a process none the less sad because it is slow and subtle. It begins in the Elizabethans in an innocent and indefinable form. It is merely the sense that, though Macbeth may get his crown crookedly, he must not actually wear it crooked. It is the sense that, though Claudius may fall from his throne, he must not actually fall over his footstool.

It ended in the nineteenth century in many refined and

ingenuous forms; in a tendency to find all fun in the ignorant or criminal classes; in dialect or the dropping of aitches. It was a sort of satirical slumming. There was a new shade in the comparison of the coster with the cat; a coster could look at a king and might conceivably laugh at a king; but most contemporary art and literature was occupied in laughing at the coster.

Even in the long lifetime of a good comic paper like *Punch* we can trace the change from jokes against the palace to jokes against the public-house. The difference is perhaps more delicate; it is rather that the refined classes are a subject for refined comedy; and only the common people a subject for common farce. It is correct to call this refinement modern; yet it is not quite correct to call it contemporary. All through the Victorian time the joke was pointed more against the poor and less against the powerful; but the revolution which ended the long Victorian peace has shaken this Victorian patronage. The great war which has brought so many ancient realities to the surface has re-enacted before our eyes the Miracle Play of Coventry.

We have seen a real King Herod claiming the thunders of the throne of God, and answered by the thunder not merely of human wrath but of primitive human laughter. He has done murder by proclamations, and he has been answered by caricatures. He has made a massacre of children, and been made a figure of fun in a Christmas pantomime for the pleasure of other children. Precisely because his crime is tragic, his punishment is comic; the old popular paradox has returned.

The Silver Goblets

IT was reported that at the sumptuous performance of *Henry VIII* at His Majesty's Theatre, the urns and goblets of the banquet were specially wrought in real and solid silver and in the style of the sixteenth century. This bombastic literalism is at least very much the fashion in our modern theatricals. Mr. Vincent Crummles considered it a splendid piece of thoroughness on the part of an actor that he should black himself all over to perform Othello. But Mr. Crummles's ideal falls far short of the theoretic thoroughness of the late Sir Herbert Tree; who would consider blacking oneself all over as comparatively a mere sham, compromise, and veneer. Sir Herbert Tree would, I suppose, send for a real negro to act Othello; and perhaps for a real Jew to act Shylock—though that, in the present condition of the English stage, might possibly be easier. The strict principle of the silver goblets might be a little more arduous and unpleasant if applied, let us say, to *The Arabian Nights*, if the manager of His Majesty's Theatre presented *Aladdin*, and had to produce not one real negro but a hundred real negroes, carrying a hundred baskets of gigantic and genuine jewels. In the presence of this proposal even Sir Herbert might fall back on a simpler philosophy of the drama. For the principle in itself admits of no limit. If once it be allowed that what looks like silver behind the footlights is better also for really being silver, there seems no reason why the wildest developments should not ensue. The priests in *Henry VIII* might be specially ordained in the green-room before they come on. Nay, if it comes to that, the head of Buckingham might really be cut off; as in the glad old days lamented by Swinburne, before the coming of an emasculate mysticism removed real death from the arena. We might re-establish the goriness as well as the gorgeousness of the amphitheatre. If real wine-cups, why not real wine? If real wine, why not real blood?

Nor is this an illegitimate or irrelevant deduction. This and a hundred other fantasies might follow if once we admit the first principle that we need to realize on the stage not merely the beauty of silver, but the value of silver. Shakespeare's famous phrase that art should hold the mirror up to nature is always taken as wholly realistic; but it is really idealistic and symbolic—at least, compared with the realism of His Majesty's. Art is a mirror not because it is the same as the object, but because it is different. A mirror selects as much as art selects; it gives the light of flames, but not their heat; the colour of flowers, but not their fragrance; the faces of women, but not their voices; the proportions of stockbrokers, but not their solidity. A mirror is a vision of things, not a working model of them. And the silver seen in a mirror is not for sale.

But the results of the thing in practice are worse than its wildest results in theory. This Arabian extravagance in the furniture and decoration of a play has one very practical disadvantage—that it narrows the number of experiments, confines them to a small and wealthy class, and makes those which are made exceptional, erratic, and unrepresentative of any general dramatic activity. One or two insanely expensive works prove nothing about the general state of art in a country. To take the parallel of a performance somewhat less dignified, perhaps, than Sir Herbert Tree's, there has lately been in America an exhibition not unanalogous to a conflict in the arena, and one for which a real negro actually was procured by the management. The negro happened to beat the white man, and both before and after this event people went about wildly talking of "the White Man's champion" and "the representative of the Black Race." All black men were supposed to have triumphed over all white men in a sort of mysterious Armageddon because one specialist met another specialist and tapped his claret or punched him in the bread-basket.

Now the fact is, of course, that these two prize-fighters were so specially picked and trained—the business of producing such men is so elaborate, artificial, and expensive—that the result proves nothing whatever about the general condition of white men or black. If you go in for heroes or monsters it is obvious that they may be born anywhere. If you took the two tallest men on earth, one might be born in Corea and the other in Camberwell, but this would not make Camberwell a land of giants inheriting the blood of Anak. If you took the two thinnest men in the world, one might be a Parisian and the other a Red Indian. And if you take the two most scientifically developed pugilists, it is not surprising that one of them should happen to be white and the other black. Experiments of so special and profuse a kind have the character of monstrosities, like black tulips or blue roses. It is absurd to make them representative of races and causes that they do not represent. You might as well say that the Bearded Lady at a fair represents the masculine advance of modern woman; or that all Europe was shaking under the banded armies of Asia, because of the co-operation of the Siamese Twins.

So the plutocratic tendency of such performances as *Henry VIII* is to prevent rather than to embody any movement of historical or theatrical imagination. If the standard of expenditure is set so high by custom, the number of competitors must necessarily be small, and will probably be of a restricted and unsatisfactory type. Instead of English history and English literature being as cheap as silver paper, they will be as dear as silver plate. The national culture, instead of being spread out everywhere like gold leaf, will be hardened into a few costly lumps of gold—and kept in very few pockets. The modern world is full of things that are theoretically open and popular, but practically private and even corrupt. In theory any tinker can be chosen to speak for his fellow-citizens among the English Commons. In practice he may have to spend a thousand pounds on getting elected—a sum which many tinkers do not happen to have to spare. In theory it ought to be possible for any moderately successful actor with a sincere and interesting conception of Wolsey to put that conception on the stage. In practice it looks as if he would have to ask himself, not whether he was as clever as Wolsey, but whether he was as rich. He has to reflect, not whether he can enter into Wolsey's soul, but whether he can pay Wolsey's servants, purchase Wolsey's plate, and own Wolsey's palaces.

Now people with Wolsey's money and people with Wolsey's mind are both rare; and even with him the mind came before the money. The chance of their being combined a second time is manifestly small and decreasing. The result will obviously be that thousands and millions may be spent on a theatrical misfit, and inappropriate and unconvincing impersonation; and all the time there may be a man outside who could have put on a red dressing-gown and made us feel in the presence of the most terrible of the Tudor statesmen. The modern method is to sell Shakespeare for thirty pieces of silver.

The Duty of the Historian

WE most of us suffer much from having learnt all our lessons in history from those little abridged history-books in use in most public and private schools. These lessons are insufficient—especially when you don't learn them. The latter was indeed my own case; and the little history I know I have picked up since by rambling about in authentic books and countrysides. But the bald summaries of the small history-books still master and, in many cases, mislead us. The root of the difficulty is this: that there are two quite distinct purposes of history—the superior purpose, which is its use for children, and the secondary or inferior purpose, which is its use for historians. The highest and noblest thing that history can be is a good story. Then it appeals to the heroic heart of all generations, the eternal infancy of mankind. Such a story as that of William Tell could literally be told of any epoch; no barbarian implements could be too rude, no scientific instruments could be too elaborate for the pride and terror of the tale. It might be told of the first flint-headed arrow or the last model machine-gun; the point of it is the same: it is as eternal as tyranny and fatherhood. Now, wherever there is this function of the fine story in history we tell it to children only because it is a fine story. David and the cup of water, Regulus and the *atque sciebat*, Jeanne d'Arc kissing the cross of spear-wood, or Nelson shot with all his stars—these stir in every child the ancient heart of his race; and that is all that they need do. Changes of costume and local colour are nothing: it did not matter that in the illustrated Bibles of our youth David was dressed rather like Regulus, in a Roman cuirass and sandals, any more than it mattered that in the illuminated Bibles of the Middle Ages he was dressed rather like Jeanne d'Arc, in a hood or a visored helmet. It will not matter to future ages if the pictures represent Jeanne d'Arc cremated in an asbestos stove or Nelson dying in a top-hat. For the childish and eternal use of history, the history will still be heroic.

But the historians have quite a different business. It is their affair, not merely to remember that humanity has been wise and great, but to understand the special ways in which it has been weak and foolish. Historians have to explain the horrible mystery of how fashions were ever fashionable. They have to analyse that statuesque instinct of the South that moulds the Roman cuirass to the muscles of the human torso, or that element of symbolic extravagance in the later Middle Ages which let loose a menagerie upon breast and casque and shield. They have to explain, as best they can, how anyone ever came to have a top-hat, how anyone ever endured an asbestos stove.

Now the mere tales of the heroes are a part of religious education; they are meant to teach us that we have souls. But the inquiries of the historians into the eccentricities of every epoch are merely a part of political education; they are meant to teach us to avoid certain perils or solve certain problems in the complexity of practical affairs. It is the first duty of a boy to admire the glory of Trafalgar. It is the first duty of a grown man to question its utility. It is one question whether it was a good thing as an episode in the struggle between Pitt and the French Revolution. It is quite another matter that it was certainly a good thing in that immortal struggle between the son of man and all the unclean spirits of sloth and cowardice and despair. For the wisdom of man alters with every age; his prudence has to fit perpetually shifting shapes of inconvenience or dilemma. But his folly is immortal: a fire stolen from heaven.

Now, the little histories that we learnt as children were partly meant simply as inspiring stories. They largely consisted of tales like Alfred and the cakes or Eleanor and the poisoned wound. They ought to have entirely consisted of them. Little children ought to learn nothing but legends; they are the beginnings of all sound morals and manners. I would not be severe on the point: I would not exclude a story solely because it was true. But the essential on which I should insist would be, not that the tale must be true, but that the tale must be fine.

The attempts in the little school-histories to introduce older and subtler elements, to talk of the atmosphere of Puritanism or the evolution of our Constitution, is quite irrelevant and vain. It is impossible to convey to a barely breeched imp who does not yet know his own community, the exquisite divergence between it and some other community. What is the good of talking about the Constitution carefully balanced on three estates to a creature only quite recently balanced on two legs? What is the sense of explaining the Puritan shade of morality to a creature who is still learning with difficulty that there is any morality at all? We may put on one side the possibility that some of us may think the Puritan atmosphere an unpleasant one or the Constitution a trifle rickety on its three legs. The general truth remains that we should teach, to the young, men's enduring truths, and let the learned amuse themselves with their passing errors.

It is often said nowadays that in great crises and moral revolutions we need one strong man to decide; but it seems to me that that is exactly when we do not need him. We do not need a great man for a revolution, for a true revolution is a time when all men are great. Where despotism really is successful is in very small matters. Every one must have noticed how essential a despot is to arranging the things in which every one is doubtful, because every one is indifferent: the boats in a water picnic or the seats at a dinner-party. Here the man who knows his own mind is really wanted, for no one else ever thinks his own mind worth knowing. No one knows where to go to precisely, because no one cares where he goes. It is for trivialities that the great tyrant is meant.

But when the depths are stirred in a society, and all men's souls grow taller in a transfiguring anger or desire, then I am by no means so certain that the great man has been a benefit even when he has appeared. I am sure that Cromwell and Napoleon managed the mere pikes and bayonets, boots and knapsacks better than most other people could have managed them. But I am by no means sure that Napoleon gave a better turn to the whole French Revolution. I am by no means so sure that Cromwell has really improved the religion of England.

As it is in politics with the specially potent man, so it is in history with the specially learned. We do not need the learned man to teach us the important things. We all know the important things, though we all violate and neglect them. Gigantic industry, abysmal knowledge, are needed for the discovery of the tiny things—the things that seem hardly worth the trouble. Generally speaking, the ordinary man should be content with the terrible secret that men are men—which is another way of saying that they are brothers. He had better think of Cæsar as a man and not as a Roman, for he will probably think of a Roman as a statue and not as a man. He had better think of Cœur-de-Lion as a man and not as a Crusader, or he will think of him as a stage Crusader. For every man knows the inmost core of every other man. It is the trappings and externals erected for an age and a fashion that are forgotten and unknown. It is all the curtains that are curtained, all the masks that are masked, all the disguises that are now disguised in dust and featureless decay. But though we cannot reach the outside of history, we all start from the inside. Some day, if I ransack whole libraries, I may know the outermost aspects of King Stephen, and almost see him in his habit as he lived; but the inmost I know already. The symbols are mouldered and the manner of the oath forgotten; the secret society may even be dissolved; but we all know the secret.

Questions of Divorce

I HAVE just picked up a little book that is not only brightly and suggestively written, but is somewhat unique, in this sense—that it enunciates the modern and advanced view of Woman in such language as a sane person can stand. It is written by Miss Florence Farr, is called *Modern Woman: her Intentions*, and is published by Mr. Frank Palmer. This style of book I confess to commonly finding foolish and vain. The New Woman's monologue wearies, not because it is unwomanly, but because it is inhuman. It exhibits the most exhausting of combinations: the union of fanaticism of speech with frigidity of soul—the things that made Robespierre seem a monster. The worst example I remember was once trumpeted in a Review: a lady doctor, who has ever afterwards haunted me as a sort of nightmare of spiritual imbecility. I forget her exact words, but they were to the effect that sex and motherhood should be treated neither with ribaldry nor reverence: "It is too serious a subject for ribaldry, and I myself cannot understand reverence towards anything that is physical." There, in a few words, is the whole twisted and tortured priggishness which poisons the present age. The person who cannot laugh at sex ought to be kicked; and the person who cannot reverence pain ought to be killed. Until that lady doctor gets a little ribaldry and a little reverence into her soul, she has no right to have any opinion at all about the affairs of humanity. I remember there was another lady, trumpeted in the same Review, a French lady who broke off her engagement with the excellent gentleman to whom she was attached on the ground that affection interrupted the flow of her thoughts. It was a thin sort of flow in any case, to judge by the samples; and no doubt it was easily interrupted.

The author of *Modern Woman* is bitten a little by the mad dog of modernity, the habit of dwelling disproportionally on the abnormal and the diseased; but she writes rationally and humorously, like a human being; she sees that there are two sides to the case; and she even puts in a fruitful suggestion that, with its subconsciousness and its virtues of the vegetable, the new psychology may turn up on the side of the old womanhood. One may say indeed that in such a book as this our amateur philosophizing of to-day is seen at its fairest; and even at its fairest it exhibits certain qualities of bewilderment and disproportion which are somewhat curious to note.

I think the oddest thing about the advanced people is that, while they are always talking of things as problems, they have hardly any notion of what a real problem is. A real problem only occurs when there are admittedly disadvantages in all courses that can be pursued. If it is discovered just before a fashionable wedding that the Bishop is locked up in the coal-cellar, that is not a problem. It is obvious to anyone but an extreme anti-clerical or practical joker that the Bishop must be let out of the coal-cellar. But suppose the Bishop has been locked up in the wine-cellar, and from the obscure noises, sounds as of song and dance, etc., it is guessed that he has indiscreetly tested the vintages round him; then, indeed, we may properly say that there has arisen a *problem*; for, upon the one hand, it is awkward to keep the wedding waiting, while, upon the other, any hasty opening of the door might mean an episcopal rush and scenes of the most unforeseen description.

An incident like this (which must constantly happen in our gay and varied social life) is a true problem because there are in it incompatible advantages. Now if woman is simply the domestic slave that many of these writers represent, if man has bound her by brute force, if he has simply knocked her down and sat on her—then there is no problem about the matter. She has been locked in the kitchen, like the Bishop in the coal-cellar; and they both of them ought to be let out. If there is any problem of sex, it must be because the case is not so simple as that; because there is something to be said for the man as well as for the woman; and because there are evils in unlocking the kitchen door, in addition to the obvious good of it. Now, I will take two instances from Miss Farr's own book of problems that are really problems, and which she entirely misses because she will not admit that they are problematical.

The writer asks the substantial question squarely enough: "Is indissoluble marriage good for mankind?" and she answers it squarely enough: "For the great mass of mankind, yes." To those like myself, who move in the old-world dream of Democracy, that admission ends the whole question. There may be exceptional people who would be happier without Civil Government; sensitive souls who really feel unwell when they see a policeman. But we have surely the right to impose the State on everybody if it suits nearly everybody; and if so, we have the right to impose the Family on everybody if it suits nearly everybody. But the queer and cogent point is this; that Miss Farr does not see the real difficulty about allowing exceptions—the real difficulty that has made most legislators reluctant to allow them. I do not say there should be no exceptions, but I do say that the author has not seen the painful problem of permitting any.

The difficulty is simply this: that if it comes to claiming exceptional treatment, the very people who will claim it will be those who least deserve it. The people who are quite convinced they are superior are the very inferior people; the men who really think themselves extraordinary are the most ordinary rotters on earth. If you say, "Nobody must steal the Crown of England," then probably it will not be stolen. After that, probably the next best thing would be to say, "Anybody may steal the Crown of England," for then the Crown might find its way to some honest and modest fellow. But if you say, "Those who feel themselves to have Wild and Wondrous Souls, and they only, may steal the Crown of England," then you may be sure there will be a rush for it of all the rag, tag, and bobtail of the universe, all the quack doctors, all the sham artists, all the demireps and drunken egotists, all the nationless adventurers and criminal monomaniacs of the world.

So, if you say that marriage is for common people, but divorce for free and noble spirits, all the weak and selfish people will dash for the divorce; while the few free and noble spirits you wish to help will very probably (because they are free and noble) go on wrestling with the marriage. For it is one of the marks of real dignity of character not to wish to separate oneself from the honour and tragedy of the whole tribe. All men are ordinary men; the extraordinary men are those who know it.

The weakness of the proposition that marriage is good for the common herd, but can be advantageously violated by special "experimenters" and pioneers, is that it takes no account of the problem of the disease of pride. It is easy enough to say that weaker souls had better be guarded, but that we must give freedom to Georges Sand or make exceptions for George Eliot. The practical puzzle is this: that it is precisely the weakest sort of lady novelist who thinks she is Georges Sand; it is precisely the silliest woman who is sure she is George Eliot. It is the small soul that is sure it is an exception; the large soul is only too proud to be the rule. To advertise for exceptional people is to collect all the sulks and sick fancies and futile ambitions of the earth. The good artist is he who can be understood; it is the bad artist who is always "misunderstood." In short, the great man is a man; it is always the tenth-rate man who is the Superman.

Miss Farr disposes of the difficult question of vows and bonds in love by leaving out altogether the one extraordinary fact of experience on which the whole matter turns. She again solves the problem by assuming that it is not a problem. Concerning oaths of fidelity, etc., she writes: "We cannot trust ourselves to make a real love-knot unless money or custom forces us to 'bear and forbear.' There is always the lurking fear that we shall not be able to keep faith unless we swear upon the Book. This is, of course, not true of young lovers. Every first love is born free of tradition; indeed, not only is first love innocent and valiant, but it sweeps aside all the wise laws it has been taught, and burns away experience in its own light. The revelation is so extraordinary, so unlike anything told by the poets, so absorbing, that it is impossible to believe that the feeling can die out."

Now this is exactly as if some old naturalist settled the bat's place in nature by saying boldly, "Bats do not fly." It is as if he solved the problem of whales by bluntly declaring that whales live on land. There is a problem of vows, as of bats and whales. What Miss Farr says about it is quite lucid and explanatory; it simply happens to be flatly untrue. It is not the fact that young lovers have no desire to swear on the Book. They are always at it. It is not the fact that every young love is born free of traditions about binding and promising, about bonds and signatures and seals. On the contrary, lovers wallow in the wildest pedantry and precision about these matters. They do the craziest things to make their love legal and irrevocable. They tattoo each other with promises; they cut into rocks and oaks with their names and vows; they bury ridiculous things in ridiculous places to be a witness against them; they bind each other with rings, and inscribe each other in Bibles; if they are raving lunatics (which is not untenable), they are mad solely on this idea of binding and on nothing else. It is quite true that the tradition of their fathers and mothers is in favour of fidelity; but it is emphatically not true that the lovers merely follow it; they invent it anew. It is quite true that the lovers feel their love eternal, and independent of oaths; but it is emphatically not true that they do not desire to take the oaths. They have a ravening thirst to take as many oaths as possible. Now this is the paradox; this is the whole problem. It is not true, as Miss Farr would have it, that young people feel free of vows, being confident of constancy; while old people invent vows, having lost that confidence. That would be much too simple; if that were so there would be no problem at all. The startling but quite solid fact is that young people are especially fierce in making fetters and final ties at the very moment when they think them unnecessary. The time when they want the vow is exactly the time when they do not need it. That is worth thinking about.

Nearly all the fundamental facts of mankind are to be found in its fables. And there is a singularly sane truth in all the old stories of the monsters—such as centaurs, mermaids, sphinxes, and the rest. It will be noted that in each of these the humanity, though imperfect in its extent, is perfect in its quality. The mermaid is half a lady and half a fish; but there is nothing fishy about the lady. A centaur is half a gentleman and half a horse. But there is nothing horsey about the gentleman. The centaur is a manly sort of man—up to a certain point. The mermaid is a womanly woman—so far as she goes. The human parts of these monsters are handsome, like heroes, or lovely, like nymphs; their bestial appendages do not affect the full perfection of their humanity—what there is of it. There is nothing humanly wrong with the centaur, except that he rides a horse without a head. There is nothing humanly wrong with the mermaid; Hood put a good comic motto to his picture of a mermaid: "All's well that ends well." It is, perhaps, quite true; it all depends which end. Those old wild images included a crucial truth. Man is a monster. And he is all the more a monster because one part of him is perfect. It is not true, as the evolutionists say, that man moves perpetually up a slope from imperfection to perfection, changing ceaselessly, so as to be suitable. The immortal part of a man and the deadly part are jarringly distinct, and have always been. And the best proof of this is in such a case as we have considered—the case of the oaths of love.

A man's soul is as full of voices as a forest; there are ten thousand tongues there like all the tongues of the trees: fancies, follies, memories, madnesses, mysterious fears, and more mysterious hopes. All the settlement and sane government of life consists in coming to the conclusion that some of those voices have authority and others not. You may have an impulse to fight your enemy or an impulse to run away from him; a reason to serve your country or a reason to betray it; a good idea for making sweets or a better idea for poisoning them. The only test I know by which to judge one argument or inspiration from another is ultimately this: that all the noble necessities of man talk the language of eternity. When man is doing the three or four things that he was sent on this earth to do, then he speaks like one who shall live for ever. A man dying for his country does not talk as if local preferences could change. Leonidas does not say, "In my present mood, I prefer Sparta to Persia." William Tell does not remark, "The Swiss civilization, so far as I can yet see, is superior to the Austrian." When men are making commonwealths, they talk in terms of the absolute, and so they do when they are making (however unconsciously) those smaller commonwealths which are called families. There are in life certain immortal moments, moments that have authority. Lovers are right to tattoo each other's skins and cut each other's names about the world; they do belong to each other, in a more awful sense than they know.

Mormonism

THERE is inevitably something comic (comic in the broad and vulgar style which all men ought to appreciate in its place) about the panic aroused by the presence of the Mormons and their supposed polygamous campaign in this country. It calls up the absurd image of an enormous omnibus, packed inside with captive English ladies, with an Elder on the box, controlling his horses with the same patriarchal gravity as his wives, and another Elder as conductor calling out "Higher up," with an exalted and allegorical intonation. And there is something highly fantastic to the ordinary healthy mind in the idea of any precaution being proposed; in the idea of locking the Duchess in the boudoir and the governess in the nursery, lest they should make a dash for Utah, and become the ninety-third Mrs. Abraham Nye, or the hundredth Mrs. Hiram Boke. But these frankly vulgar jokes, like most vulgar jokes, cover a popular prejudice which is but the bristly hide of a living principle. Elder Ward, recently speaking at Nottingham, strongly protested against these rumours, and asserted absolutely that polygamy had never been practised with the consent of the Mormon Church since 1890. I think it only just that this disclaimer should be circulated; but though it is most probably sincere, I do not find it very soothing. The year 1890 is not very long ago, and a society that could have practised so recently a custom so alien to Christendom must surely have a moral attitude which might be repellent to us in many other respects. Moreover, the phrase about the consent of the Church (if correctly reported) has a little the air of an official repudiating responsibility for unofficial excesses. It sounds almost as if Mr. Abraham Nye might, on his own account, come into church with a hundred and fourteen wives, but people were supposed not to notice them. It might amount to little more than this, that the chief Elder may allow the hundred and fourteen wives to walk down the street like a girls' school, but he is not officially expected to take off his hat to each of them in turn. Seriously speaking, however, I have little doubt that Elder Ward speaks the substantial truth, and that polygamy is dying, or has died, among the Mormons. My reason for thinking this is simple: it is that polygamy always tends to die out. Even in the East I believe that, counting heads, it is by this time the exception rather than the rule. Like slavery, it is always being started, because of its obvious conveniences. It has only one small inconvenience, which is that it is intolerable.

Our real error in such a case is that we do not know or care about the creed itself, from which a people's customs, good or bad, will necessarily flow. We talk much about "respecting" this or that person's religion; but the way to respect a religion is to treat it as a religion: to ask what are its tenets and what are their consequences. But modern tolerance is deafer than intolerance. The old religious authorities, at least, defined a heresy before they condemned it, and read a book before they burned it. But we are always saying to a Mormon or a Moslem—"Never mind about your religion, come to my arms." To which he naturally replies—"But I do mind about my religion, and I advise you to mind your eye."

About half the history now taught in schools and colleges is made windy and barren by this narrow notion of leaving out the theological theories. The wars and Parliaments of the Puritans made absolutely no sense if we leave out the fact that Calvinism appeared to them to be the absolute metaphysical truth, unanswerable, unreplaceable, and the only thing worth having in the world. The Crusades and dynastic quarrels of the Norman and Angevin Kings make absolutely no sense if we leave out the fact that these men (with all their vices) were enthusiastic for the doctrine, discipline, and endowment of Catholicism. Yet I have read a history of the Puritans by a modern Nonconformist in which the name of Calvin was not even mentioned, which is like writing a history of the Jews without mentioning either Abraham or Moses. And I have never read any popular or educational history of England that gave the slightest hint of the motives in the human mind that covered England with abbeys and Palestine with banners. Historians seem to have completely forgotten the two facts—first, that men act from ideas; and second, that it might, therefore, be as well to discover which ideas. The mediævals did not believe primarily in "chivalry," but in Catholicism, as producing chivalry among other things. The Puritans did not believe primarily in "righteousness," but in Calvinism, as producing righteousness among other things. It was the creed that held the coarse or cunning men of the world at both epochs. William the Conqueror was in some ways a cynical and brutal soldier, but he did attach importance to the fact that the Church upheld his enterprise; that Harold had sworn falsely on the bones of saints, and that the banner above his own lances had been blessed by the Pope. Cromwell was in some ways a cynical and brutal soldier; but he did attach importance to the fact that he had gained assurance from on high in the Calvinistic scheme; that the Bible seemed to support him—in short, the most important moment in his own life, for him, was not when Charles I lost his head, but when Oliver Cromwell did not lose his soul. If you leave these things out of the story, you are leaving out the story itself. If William Rufus was only a red-haired man who liked hunting, why did he force Anselm's head under a mitre, instead of forcing his head under a headsman's axe? If John Bunyan only cared for "righteousness," why was he in terror of being damned, when he knew he was rationally righteous? We shall never make anything of moral and religious movements in history until we begin to look at their theory as well as their practice. For their practice (as in the case of the Mormons) is often so unfamiliar and frantic that it is quite unintelligible without their theory.

I have not the space, even if I had the knowledge, to describe the fundamental theories of Mormonism about the universe. But they are extraordinarily interesting; and a proper understanding of them would certainly enable us to see daylight through the more perplexing or menacing customs of this community; and therefore to judge how far polygamy was in their scheme a permanent and self-renewing principle or (as is quite probable) a personal and unscrupulous accident. The basic Mormon belief is one that comes out of the morning of the earth, from the most primitive and even infantile attitude. Their chief dogma is that God is material, not that He was materialized once, as all Christians believe; nor that He is materialized specially, as all Catholics believe; but that He was materially embodied from all time; that He has a local habitation as well as a name. Under the influence of this barbaric but violently vivid conception, these people crossed a great desert with their guns and oxen, patiently, persistently, and courageously, as if they were following a vast and visible giant who was striding across the plains. In other words, this strange sect, by soaking itself solely in the Hebrew Scriptures, had really managed to reproduce the atmosphere of those Scriptures as they are felt by Hebrews rather than by Christians. A number of dull, earnest, ignorant, black-coated men with chimney-pot hats, chin beards or mutton-chop whiskers, managed to reproduce in their own souls the richness and the peril of an ancient Oriental experience. If we think from this end we may possibly guess how it was that they added polygamy.

Pageants and Dress

THE only objection to the excellent series of Pageants that has adorned England of late is that they are made too expensive. The mass of the common people cannot afford to see the Pageant; so they are obliged to put up with the inferior function of acting in it. I myself got in with the rabble in this way. It was to the Church Pageant; and I was much impressed with certain illuminations which such an experience makes possible. A Pageant exhibits all the fun of a Fancy Dress Ball, with this great difference: that its motive is reverent instead of irreverent. In the one case a man dresses up as his great-grandfather in order to make game of his great-grandfather; in the other case, in order to do him honour. What the great-grandfather himself would think of either of them we fortunately have not to conjecture. The alteration is important and satisfactory. All natural men regard their ancestors as dignified because they are dead; it was a great pity and folly that we had fallen into the habit of regarding the Middle Ages as a mere second-hand shop for comic costumes. Mediæval costume and heraldry had been meant as the very manifestation of courage and publicity and a decent pride. Colours were worn that they might be conspicuous across a battle-field; an animal was rampant on a helmet that he might stand up evident against the sky. The mediæval time has been talked of too much as if it were full of twilight and secrecies. It was a time of avowal and of what many modern people call vulgarity. A man's dress was that of his family or his trade or his religion; and these are exactly the three things which we now think it bad taste to discuss. Imagine a modern man being dressed in green and orange because he was a Robinson. Or imagine him dressed in blue and gold because he was an auctioneer. Or imagine him dressed in purple and silver because he was an agnostic. He is now dressed only in the ridiculous disguise of a gentleman; which tells one nothing at all, not even whether he is one. If ever he dresses up as a cavalier or a monk it is only as a joke—very often as a disreputable and craven joke, a joke in a mask. That vivid and heraldic costume which was meant to show everybody who a man was is now chiefly worn by people at Covent Garden masquerades who wish to conceal who they are. The clerk dresses up as a monk in order to be absurd. If the monk dressed up as a clerk in order to be absurd I could understand it; though the escapade might disturb his monastic superiors. A man in a sensible gown and hood might possibly put on a top-hat and a pair of trousers in order to cover himself with derision, in some extravagance of mystical humility. But that a man who calmly shows himself to the startled sky every morning in a top-hat and trousers should think it comic to put on a simple and dignified robe and hood is a situation which almost splits the brain. Things like the Church Pageant may do something towards snubbing this silly and derisive view of the past. Hitherto the young stockbroker, when he wanted to make a fool of himself, dressed up as Cardinal Wolsey. It may now begin to dawn on him that he ought rather to make a wise man of himself before attempting the impersonation.

Nevertheless, the truth which the Pageant has to tell the British public is rather more special and curious than one might at first assume. It is easy enough to say in the rough that modern dress is dingy, and that the dress of our fathers was more bright and picturesque. But that is not really the point. At Fulham Palace one can compare the huge crowd of people acting in the Pageant with the huge crowd of people looking at it. There is a startling difference, but it is not a mere difference between gaiety and gloom. There is many a respectable young woman in the audience who has on her own hat more colours than the whole Pageant put together. There are belts of brown and black in the Pageant itself: the Puritans round the scaffold of Laud, or the black-robed doctors of the eighteenth century. There are patches of purple and yellow in the audience: the more select young ladies and the less select young gentlemen. It is not that our age has no appetite for the gay or the gaudy—it is a very hedonistic age. It is not that past ages—even the rich symbolic Middle Ages—did not feel any sense of safety in what is sombre or restrained. A friar in a brown coat is much more severe than an 'Arry in a brown bowler. Why is it that he is also much more pleasant?

I think the whole difference is in this: that the first man is brown with a reason and the second without a reason. If a hundred monks wore one brown habit it was because they felt that their toil and brotherhood were well expressed in being clad in the coarse, dark colour of the earth. I do not say that they said so, or even clearly thought so; but their artistic instinct went straight when they chose the mud-colour for laborious brethren or the flame-colour for the first princes of the Church. But when 'Arry puts on a brown bowler he does not either with his consciousness or his subconsciousness (that rich soil) feel that he is crowning his brows with the brown earth, clasping round his temples a strange crown of clay. He does not wear a dust-coloured hat as a form of strewing dust upon his head. He wears a dust-coloured hat because the nobility and gentry who are his models discourage him from wearing a crimson hat or a golden hat or a peacock-green hat. He is not thinking of the brownness of brown. It is not to him a symbol of the roots, of realism, or of autochthonous humility; on the contrary, he thinks it looks rather "classy."

The modern trouble is not that the people do not see splendid colours or striking effects. The trouble is that they see too much of them and see them divorced from all reason. It is a misfortune of modern language that the word "insignificant" is vaguely associated with the words "small" or "slight." But a thing is insignificant when we do not know what it signifies. An African elephant lying dead in Ludgate Circus would be insignificant. That is, one could not recognize it as the sign or message of anything. One could not regard it as an allegory or a love-token. One could not even call it a hint. In the same way the solar system is insignificant. Unless you have some special religious theory of what it means, it is merely big and silly, like the elephant in Ludgate Circus. And similarly, modern life, with its vastness, its energy, its elaboration, its wealth, is, in the exact sense, insignificant. Nobody knows what we mean; we do not know ourselves. Nobody could explain intelligently why a coat is black, why a waistcoat is white, why asparagus is eaten with the fingers, or why Hammersmith omnibuses are painted red. The mediævals had a much stronger idea of crowding all possible significance into things. If they had consented to waste red paint on a large and ugly Hammersmith omnibus it would have been in order to suggest that there was some sort of gory magnanimity about Hammersmith. A heraldic lion is no more like a real lion than a chimney-pot hat is like a chimney-pot. But the lion was meant to be a lion. And the chimney-pot hat was not meant to be like a chimney-pot or like anything else. The resemblance only struck certain philosophers (probably gutter-boys) afterwards. The top-hat was not intended as a high uncastellated tower; it was not intended at all. This is the real baseness of modernity. This is, for example, the only real vulgarity of advertisements. It is not that the colours on the posters are bad. It is that they are much too good for the meaningless work which they serve. When at last people see— as at the Pageant—crosses and dragons, leopards and lilies, there is scarcely one of the things that they now see as a symbol which they have not already seen as a trade-mark. If the great "Assumption of the Virgin" were painted in front of them they might remember Blank's Blue. If the Emperor of China were buried before them, the yellow robes might remind them of Dash's Mustard. We have not the task of preaching colour and gaiety to a people that has never had it, to Puritans who have neither seen nor appreciated it. We have a harder task. We have to teach those to appreciate it who have always seen it.

On Stage Costume

WHILE watching the other evening a very well-managed reproduction of *A Midsummer Night's Dream*, I had the sudden conviction that the play would be much better if it were acted in modern costume, or, at any rate, in English costume. We all remember hearing in our boyhood about the absurd conventionality of Garrick and Mrs. Siddons, when he acted Macbeth in a tie-wig and a tail-coat, and she acted Lady Macbeth in a crinoline as big and stiff as a cartwheel. This has always been talked of as a piece of comic ignorance or impudent modernity; as if Rosalind appeared in rational dress with a bicycle; as if Portia appeared with a horsehair wig and side-whiskers. But I am not so sure that the great men and women who founded the English stage in the eighteenth century were quite such fools as they looked; especially as they looked to the romantic historians and eager archæologists of the nineteenth century. I have a queer suspicion that Garrick and Siddons knew nearly as much about dressing as they did about acting.

One distinction can at least be called obvious. Garrick did not care much for the historical costume of Macbeth; but he cared as much as Shakespeare did. He did not know much about that prehistoric and partly mythical Celtic chief; but he knew more than Shakespeare; and he could not conceivably have cared less. Now the Victorian age was honestly interested in the dark and epic origins of Europe; was honestly interested in Picts and Scots, in Celts and Saxons; in the blind drift of the races and the blind drive of the religions. Ossian and the Arthurian revival had interested people in distant dark-headed men who probably never existed. Freeman, Carlyle, and the other Teutonists had interested them in distant fair-headed men who almost certainly never existed. Pusey and Pugin and the first High Churchmen had interested them in shaven-headed men, dark or fair, men who did undoubtedly exist, but whose real merits and defects would have startled their modern admirers very considerably. Under these circumstances it is not strange that our age should have felt a curiosity about the solid but mysterious Macbeth of the Dark Ages. But all this does not alter the ultimate fact: that the only Macbeth that mankind will ever care about is the Macbeth of Shakespeare, and not the Macbeth of history. When England was romantic it was interested in Macbeth's kilt and claymore. In the same way, if England becomes a Republic, it will be specially interested in the Republicans in *Julius Cæsar*. If England becomes Roman Catholic, it will be specially interested in the theory of chastity in *Measure for Measure*. But being interested in these things will never be the same as being interested in Shakespeare. And for a man interested in Shakespeare, a man merely concerned about what Shakespeare meant, a Macbeth in powdered hair and knee-breeches is perfectly satisfactory. For Macbeth, as Shakespeare shows him, is much more like a man in knee-breeches than a man in a kilt. His subtle hesitations and his suicidal impenitence belong to the bottomless speculations of a highly civilized society. The "Out, out, brief candle" is far more appropriate to the last wax taper after a ball of powder and patches than to the smoky but sustained fires in iron baskets which probably flared and smouldered over the swift crimes of the eleventh century. The real Macbeth probably killed Duncan with the nearest weapon, and then confessed it to the nearest priest. Certainly, he may never have had any such doubts about the normal satisfaction of being alive. However regrettably negligent of the importance of Duncan's life, he had, I fancy, few philosophical troubles about the importance of his own. The men of the Dark Ages were all optimists, as all children and all animals are. The madness of Shakespeare's Macbeth goes along with candles and silk stockings. That madness only appears in the age of reason.

So far, then, from Garrick's anachronism being despised, I should like to see it imitated. Shakespeare got the tale of Theseus from Athens, as he got the tale of Macbeth from Scotland; and having reluctantly seen the names of those two countries in the record, I am convinced that he never gave them another thought. Macbeth is not a Scotchman; he is a man. But Theseus is not only not an Athenian; he is actually and unmistakably an Englishman. He is the Super-Squire; the best version of the English country gentleman; better than Wardle in *Pickwick*. The Duke of Athens is a duke (that is, a dook), but not of Athens. That free city is thousands of miles away.

If Theseus came on the stage in gaiters or a shooting-jacket, if Bottom the Weaver wore a smock-frock, if Hermia and Helena were dressed as two modern English schoolgirls, we should not be departing from Shakespeare, but rather returning to him. The cold, classical draperies (of which he probably never dreamed, but with which we drape Ægisthus or Hippolyta) are not only a nuisance, but a falsehood. They misrepresent the whole meaning of the play. For the meaning of the play is that the little things of life as well as the great things stray on the borderland of the unknown. That as a man may fall among devils for a morbid crime, or fall among angels for a small piece of piety or pity, so also he may fall among fairies through an amiable flirtation or a fanciful jealousy. The fact that a back door opens into elfland is all the more reason for keeping the foreground familiar, and even prosaic. For even the fairies are very neighbourly and firelight fairies; therefore the human beings ought to be very human in order to effect the fantastic contrast. And in Shakespeare they are very human. Hermia the vixen and Helena the maypole are obviously only two excitable and quite modern girls. Hippolyta has never been an Amazon; she may perhaps have once been a Suffragette. Theseus is a gentleman, a thing entirely different from a Greek oligarch. That golden good-nature which employs culture itself to excuse the clumsiness of the uncultured is a thing quite peculiar to those lazier Christian countries where the Christian gentleman has been evolved:

> For nothing in this world can be amiss
> When simpleness and duty tender it.

Or, again, in that noble scrap of sceptical magnanimity which was unaccountably cut out in the last performance:

> The best in this kind are but
> shadows; and the worst are no
> worse if imagination amend
> them.

These are obviously the easy and reconciling comments of some kindly but cultivated squire, who will not pretend to his guests that the play is good, but who will not let the actors see that he thinks it bad. But this is certainly not the way in which an Athenian Tory like Aristophanes would have talked about a bad play.

But as the play is dressed and acted at present, the whole

idea is inverted. We do not seem to creep out of a human house into a natural wood and there find the superhuman and supernatural. The mortals, in their tunics and togas, seem more distant from us than the fairies in their hoods and peaked caps. It is an anticlimax to meet the English elves when we have already encountered the Greek gods. The same mistake, oddly enough, was made in the only modern play worth mentioning in the same street with *A Midsummer Night's Dream*, *Peter Pan*. Sir James Barrie ought to have left out the fairy dog who puts the children to bed. If children had such dogs as that they would never wish to go to fairyland.

This fault or falsity in *Peter Pan* is, of course, repeated in the strange and ungainly incident of the father being chained up in the dog's kennel. Here, indeed, it is much worse: for the manlike dog was pretty and touching: the doglike man was ignominious and repulsive. But the fallacy is the same; it is the fallacy that weakens the otherwise triumphant poetry and wit of Sir James Barrie's play; and weakens all our treatment of fairy plays at present. Fairyland is a place of positive realities, plain laws, and a decisive story. The actors of *A Midsummer Night's Dream* seemed to think that the play was meant to be chaotic. The clowns thought they must be always clowning. But in reality it is the solemnity—nay, the conscientiousness—of the yokels that is akin to the mystery of the landscape and the tale.

The Yule Log and the Democrat

A BLASTING sneer has stricken me from time to time, to the effect that I believe in the Fireside Woman. For that matter, in the present season, I believe very much in the Fireside Man. But the very word selected for this withering insinuation shows the shallowness of the philosophy which prompts it. Surely there could not be a more stunted stupidity than the suggestion that a thing must be mild and monotonous because it has to do with fire. Why should the woman be tame because she is nearest to the wildest thing in the world? It is much more absurd to say it is prosaic to live by the fireside, than to say it is prosaic to live upon the edge of a precipice. It is tenable that some people would be prosaic anywhere; but it is not the fault of the precipice. It would sound paradoxical even in a fairy-tale to say that a princess was always yawning with ennui because she was introduced to a golden griffin or a crimson dragon; and in the round of daily fact, fire is about the nearest thing to a dragon that we know. Those who cannot get a fairy-tale out of the fire will not get it out of anything else. It may be affirmed, with fair certainty, that the people who talk most scornfully about the Fireside Woman do not get it at all, and do not wish her to get it at all. Herein lies all the absurdity of the alternatives to domesticity paraded by our progressive friends.

I am not speaking, of course, of work that must be done, especially in abnormal times; I am speaking of the psychology of tedium and of the romance of life. It is apparently demanded that the fire should be concealed in the entrails of an engine; that it should work through a labyrinth of bolts and bars; that it should litter around it numberless dreary offices, and leave behind it a train of indirect and mechanical servants, each further than the last from the least faint vibration of the original energy. Then, if in some outlying shed a woman has to stand counting tickets, or tying up parcels from morning till night, that woman is supposed to be free. She has Burst the Fetters. She is Living Her Own Life. But there is supposed to be nothing but dullness for the woman who is face to face with that elemental fury which drives and fashions the whole. There is nothing poetical (as compared with the tickets and labels) in the woman who repeats the primordial adventure of Prometheus.

And there is nothing artistic (as compared with the shed) about the terrestrial light which turns the greyest room to gold; which reclothes the woman's raggedest children round the hearth with the colours of a company of Fra Angelico, so that the mere reflections of the flame can conquer the solid hues of drab and dust, and all her household is clothed with scarlet.

The fire is in this, perhaps, the finest and simplest symbol of a truth persistently misunderstood. These elementary things, the land, the roof, the family, may seem mean and miserable; and in a cynical civilization very probably will seem mean and miserable. But the things themselves are not mean or miserable; and any reformer who says they are is not only taking hold of the stick by the wrong end, he is cutting off the branch by which he is hanging. The stamp of social failure is not that men have these simple things, but, rather, that they do not have them; or even when they do, do not know that they have them. If the Fireside Woman is dull, it is because she never looks at the fire. It is because she is not, in the wise and philosophical sense, enough of a fire-worshipper. And she lacks this faculty because the whole drift of the modern world discourages that creative concentration, that intensive cultivation of the fancy, which filled the lives of our fathers with crowds of little household gods, and which created all the lesser and lighter sanctities that surround Christmas.

Amid the wild and wandering adventures of the fireside are some which made possible the very scientific progress which is prone to carp at it. The engine, of which I spoke recently, was (we have all been told) suggested because James Watt looked at the kettle. I will not conceal a suspicion that our society might have evolved better if he had looked at the fire. I mean, of course, if he had not only looked at it, but seen it, which is not always the same thing. If he had seen what there is to be seen, he might possibly have done many things. He might, for instance, have revived the Trade Guilds of Glasgow, which failed to grasp his discovery; he might have taught them to take hold of the new energy and turn it towards democracy, instead of going off and handing over his invention to the Capitalists. For the defect which betrayed all Watt's school and generation, full as it was of a virile and thrifty Radicalism, was precisely that it did not draw from these primal sources of piety and poetry. It was not sufficiently religious, and, therefore, not sufficiently domestic; and the rich rode it down at last. For the hearth is the only possible altar of insurrection, as even the pagans knew; from that fire alone are taken the flaming brands which can really lay waste the wicked cities. The truth can be told well enough by saying that James Watt would not really have comprehended the word Christmas; and would have been much annoyed if told to consider the Yule log instead of the kettle. He was the Fireside Man; but he was not domestic enough to be dangerous. For it is the domestic man and not the wild man, just as it is the domestic dog and not the wild dog, who really fights with thieves and dies at his post. There has not been a genuine popular war in England since the war of Wat Tyler, and the origin of that, it will be remembered, was strictly domestic. It was so domestic that it would not happen at all in the modern world: Wat Tyler would simply be automatically shot into prison for resisting a rational and necessary scientific inspection. It was the growth of an unhuman and unhomelike philosophy that made all the difference between the Wat of the fourteenth century and the Watt of the nineteenth. And the spirit of real democracy will not re-emerge until it rises from the fireside and comes forth in the red reality of fire; the giant of Christmas brandishing the Yule log for a club.

But there is another feature in the flaming hearth which illustrates its natural kinship with Christmas. It is a *place*, as Christmas is a time; and these vivid limitations are vital to man as a mystic. It is not merely that the idea of everything being in its right place makes all the difference between a fire in a house and a house on fire. It is that the fireplace is a frame; and it is the frame that creates the picture. By being tied to a special spot the sacred dragon becomes more powerful and, in the high imaginative sense, more free. This is that link between hearths and altars which the heathen felt, and of which I have already spoken. If the household be the heart of politics, the fire is the heart of the household; and the vital organ is spread equally everywhere only in the very low organisms. The universe of the mere universalist is one of the very low organisms. The theosophic generalizations about Nirvana and the All may be compared to the American fashion of abolishing the fireplace altogether and heating the whole house artificially to the same temperature—a depressing habit. I can imagine that a system of hot-water pipes might satisfy a Pantheist; the notion suggests a rather dreary parody of Pan and his pipes. I can imagine that a Buddhist might want his whole house warmed like the palm-house at Kew; but, I think, a limited and localized fire will always be as much associated with Christians as it has always been associated with Christmas.

Shakespeare, himself like a large and liberal fire round which winter tales are told, has hit the mark in this matter exactly, as it concerns the poet or maker of fictive things. Shakespeare does not say that the poet loses himself in the All, that he dissipates concrete things into a cloudy twilight, that he turns this home of ours into a vista or any vaguer thing. He says the exact opposite. It is "a local habitation and a name" that the poet gives to what would otherwise be nothing. This seeming narrowness which men complain of in the altar and the hearth is as broad as Shakespeare and the whole human imagination, and should command the respect even of those who think the cult of Christmas really is all imagination. Even those who can only regard the great story of Bethlehem as a fairy-tale told by the fire will yet agree that such narrowness is the first artistic necessity even of a good fairy-tale. But there are others who think, at least, that their thought strikes deeper and pierces to a more subtle truth in the mind. There are others for whom all our fairy-tales, and even all our appetite for fairy-tales, draw their fire from one central fairy-tale, as all forgeries draw their significance from a signature. They believe that this fable is a fact, and that the other fables cannot really be appreciated even as fables until we know it is a fact. For them, personality is a step beyond universality; one might almost call it an escape from universality. And what they follow is as much something more than Pantheism as a flame is something more than a temperature. For them, God is not bound down and limited by being merely everything; He is also at liberty to be something. And for them Christmas will always deal with a reality exactly as Shakespeare's poetry deals with an unreality; it will give, not to airy nothing, but to the enormous and overwhelming everything, a local habitation and a Name.

More Thoughts on Christmas

MOST sensible people say that adults cannot be expected to appreciate Christmas as much as children appreciate it. At least, Mr. G. S. Street said so, who is the most sensible man now writing in the English language. But I am not sure that even sensible people are always right; and this has been my principal reason for deciding to be silly—a decision that is now irrevocable. It may be only because I am silly, but I rather think that, relatively to the rest of the year, I enjoy Christmas more than I did when I was a child. Of course, children do enjoy Christmas—they enjoy almost everything except actually being smacked: from which truth the custom no doubt arose. But the real point is not whether a schoolboy would enjoy Christmas. The point is that he would also enjoy No Christmas. Now I say most emphatically that I should denounce, detest, abominate, and abjure the insolent institution of No Christmas. The child is glad to find a new ball, let us say, which Uncle William (dressed as St. Nicholas in everything except the halo) has put in his stocking. But if he had no new ball, he would make a hundred new balls out of the snow. And for them he would be indebted not to Christmas, but to winter. I suppose snowballing is being put down by the police, like every other Christian custom. No more will a prosperous and serious City man have a large silver star splashed suddenly on his waistcoat, veritably investing him with the Order of the Star of Bethlehem. For it is the star of innocence and novelty, and should remind him that a child can still be born. But indeed, in one sense, we may truly say the children enjoy no seasons, because they enjoy all. I myself am of the physical type that greatly prefers cold weather to hot; and I could more easily believe that Eden was at the North Pole than anywhere in the Tropics. It is hard to define the effect of weather: I can only say that all the rest of the year I am untidy, but in summer I feel untidy. Yet although (according to the modern biologists) my hereditary human body must have been of the same essential type in my boyhood as in my present decrepitude, I can distinctly remember hailing the idea of freedom and even energy on days that were quite horribly hot. It was the excellent custom at my school to give the boys a half-holiday when it seemed too hot for working. And I can well remember the gigantic joy with which I left off reading Virgil and began to run round and round a field. My tastes in this matter have changed. Nay, they have been reversed. If I now found myself (by some process I cannot easily conjecture) on a burning summer day running round and round a field, I hope I shall not appear pedantic if I say I should prefer to be reading Virgil.

And thus it is really possible, from one point of view, for elderly gentlemen to frolic at Christmas more than children can. They may really come to find Christmas more entertaining, as they have come to find Virgil more entertaining. And, in spite of all the talk about the coldness of classicism, the poet who wrote about the man who in his own country home fears neither King nor crowd was not by any means incapable of understanding Mr. Wardle. And it is exactly those sentiments, and similar ones, that the adult does appreciate better than the child. The adult, for instance, appreciates domesticity better than the child. And one of the pillars and first principles of domesticity, as Mr. Belloc has rightly pointed out, is the institution of private property. The Christmas pudding represents the mature mystery of property; and the proof of it is in the eating.

I have always held that Peter Pan was wrong. He was a charming boy, and sincere in his adventurousness; but though he was brave like a boy, he was also a coward—like a boy. He admitted it would be a great adventure to die; but it did not seem to occur to him that it would be a great adventure to live. If he had consented to march with the fraternity of his fellow-creatures, he would have found that there were solid experiences and important revelations even in growing up. They are realities which could not possibly have been made real to him without wrecking the real good in his own juvenile point of view. But that is exactly why he ought to have done as he was told. That is the only argument for parental authority. In dealing with childhood, we have a right to command it—because we should kill the childhood if we convinced it.

Now the mistake of Peter Pan is the mistake of the new theory of life. I might call it Peter Pantheism. It is the notion that there is *no* advantage in striking root. Yet, if you talk intelligently to the nearest tree, the tree will tell you that you are an unobservant ass. There is an advantage in root; and the name of it is fruit. It is not true that the nomad is even freer than the peasant. The Bedouin may rush past on his camel, leaving a whirl of dust; but dust is not free because it flies. Neither is the nomad free because he flies. You cannot grow cabbages on a camel, any more than in a condemned cell. Moreover, I believe camels commonly walk in a comparatively leisurely manner. Anyhow, most merely nomadic creatures do, for it is a great nuisance to "carry one's house with one." Gipsies do it; so do snails; but neither of them travel very fast. I inhabit one of the smallest houses that can be conceived by the cultivated classes; but I frankly confess I should be sorry to carry it with me whenever I went out for a walk. It is true that some motorists almost live in their motor-cars. But it gratifies me to state that these motorists generally die in their motor-cars too. They perish, I am pleased to say, in a startling and horrible manner, as a judgment on them for trying to outstrip creatures higher than themselves—such as the gipsy and the snail. But, broadly speaking, a house is a thing that stands still. And a thing that stands still is a thing that strikes root. One of the things that strike root is Christmas: and another is middle-age. The other great pillar of private life besides property is marriage; but I will not deal with it here. Suppose a man has neither wife nor child: suppose he has only a good servant, or only a small garden, or only a small house, or only a small dog. He will still find he has struck unintentional root. He realizes there is something in his own garden that was not even in the Garden of Eden; and therefore is not (I kiss my hand to the Socialists) in Kew Gardens or in Kensington Gardens. He realizes, what Peter Pan could not be made to realize, that a plain human house of one's own, standing in one's own backyard, is really quite as romantic as a rather cloudy house at the top of a tree or a highly conspiratorial house underneath the roots of it. But this is because he has explored his own house, which Peter Pan and such discontented children seldom do. All the same, the children ought to think of the Never-Never Land—the world that is outside. But we ought to think of the Ever-Ever Land— the world which is inside, and the world which will last. And that is why, wicked as we are, we know most about Christmas.

Dickens Again

I AM sorry that the comic costume festival which was organized for Christmas by one of the chief Dickensian societies has unavoidably fallen through. It is not for me to reproach those traitors who found it impossible to turn up: for I was one of those traitors myself. Whatever character it was that I was expected to appear in—Jingle, I suppose, or possibly Uriah Heep—was, under a final press of business, refused by me. These Dickensian enthusiasts were going to have a Christmas party at Rochester, where they would brew punch and drink punch, and drive coaches and fall off coaches, and do all the proper Pickwickian things. How many of them were ready to make a hole in the ice, to be wheeled about in a wheelbarrow, or to wait all night outside a ladies' school, the official documents have not informed me. But I would gladly take a moderate part. I could not brew punch for the Pickwick Club; but I could drink it. I could not drive the coach for the Pickwick Club—or, indeed, for any club except the Suicide Club; but I could fall off the coach amid repeated applause and enthusiastic encores. I should be only too proud if it could be said of me, as of Sam's hyperbolical old gentleman who was tipped into the hyperbolical canal, that "'is 'at was found, but I can't be certain 'is 'ead was in it." It seems to me like a euthanasia: more beautiful than the passing of Arthur.

But though the failure of this particular festivity was merely accidental (like my own unfortunate fall off the coach), it is not without its parallel in the present position of Dickensians and Christmas. For the truth is that we simply cannot recreate the Pickwick Club—unless we have a moral basis as sturdy as that of Dickens, and even a religious basis as sturdy as that of Christmas. Men at such a time turn their backs to the solemn thing they are celebrating, as the horses turn their backs to the coach. But they are pulling the coach. And the best of it is this: that so long as the Christmas feast had some kind of assumed and admitted meaning, it was praised, and praised sympathetically, by the great men whom we should call most unsympathetic with it. That Shakespeare and Dickens and Walter Scott should write of it seems quite natural. They were people who would be as welcome at Christmas as Santa Claus.

But I do not think many people have ever wished they could ask Milton to eat the Christmas pudding. Nevertheless, it is quite certain that his Christmas ode is not only one of the richest but one of the most human of his masterpieces. I do not think that anyone specially wanting a rollicking article on Christmas would desire, by mere instinct, the literary style of Addison. Yet it is quite certain that the somewhat difficult task of really liking Addison is rendered easier by his account of the Coverley Christmas than by anything else he wrote. I even go so far as to doubt whether one of the little Cratchits (who stuffed their spoons in their mouths lest they should scream for goose) would have removed the spoon to say, "Oh, that Tennyson were here!" Yet certainly Tennyson's spirits do seem to revive in a more or less real way at the ringing of the Christmas bells in the most melancholy part of *In Memoriam*. These great men were not trying to be merry: some of them, indeed, were trying to be miserable. But the day itself was too strong for them; the time was more than their temperaments; the tradition was alive. The festival was roaring in the streets, so that prigs and even prophets (who are sometimes worse still) were honestly carried off their feet.

The difficulty with Dickens is not any failure in Dickens, nor even in the popularity of Dickens. On the contrary, he has recaptured his creative reputation and fascination far more than any of the other great Victorians. Macaulay, who was really great in his way, is rejected; Cobbett, who was much greater, is forgotten. Dickens is not merely alive: he is risen from the dead. But the difficulty is in the failing under his feet, as it were, of that firm historic platform on which he had performed his Christmas pantomimes: a platform of which he was quite as unconscious as we, most of us, are of the floor we walk about on. The fact is that the fun of Christmas is founded on the seriousness of Christmas; and to pull away the latter support even from under a Christmas clown is to let him down through a trap-door. And even clowns do not like the trap-doors that they do not expect. Thus it is unfortunately true that so glorious a thing as a Pickwick party tends to lose the splendid quality of a mere Mummery, and become that much more dull and conventional thing, a Covent Garden Ball. We are not ourselves living in the proper spirit of Pickwick. We are pretending to be old Dickens characters, when we ought to be new Dickens characters in reality.

The conditions are further complicated by the fact that while reading Dickens may make a man Dickensian, studying Dickens makes him quite the reverse. One might as well expect the aged custodian of a museum of sculpture to look (and dress) like the Apollo Belvedere, as expect the Pickwickian qualities in those literary critics who are attracted by the Dickens fiction as the materials for a biography or the subject of a controversy; as a mass of detail; as a record and a riddle. Those who study such things are a most valuable class of the community, and they do good service to Dickens in their own way. But their type and temperament are not, in the nature of things, likely to be full of the festive magic of their master. Take, for example, these endless discussions about the proper ending of *Edwin Drood*. I thought Mr. William Archer's contributions to the query some time ago were particularly able and interesting; but I could not, with my hand on my heart, call Mr. William Archer a festive gentleman, or one supremely fitted to follow Mr. Swiveller as Perpetual Grand of the Glorious Apollos. Or again, I see that Sir William Robertson Nicoll has been writing on the same Drood mystery; and I know that his knowledge of Victorian literature is both vast and exact. But I hardly think that a Puritan Scot with a sharp individualistic philosophy would be the right person to fall off the coach. Sir William Nicoll, if I remember right, once forcibly described his individualist philosophy as "firing out the fools." And certainly the spirit of Dickens could be best described as the delight in firing them in. It is exactly because Christmas is not only a feast of children, but in some sense a feast of fools, that Dickens is in touch with its mystery.

Taffy

I DO not understand Welshmen. When we say we do not understand such-and-such a person, we usually mean that he has been making himself a nuisance. He has been bothering us in some way; and the puzzle of his motives and further intentions has become a practical one. I do not mean anything of the kind here: I mean barely what I say. The distant Trojans never injured me. Taffy never came to my house or stole any part of the provisions. On the contrary, historically speaking, I went to Taffy's house and took away a good deal of what belonged to him. I do not think that Taffy is a thief; I do not even know enough about him to be sure of the preliminary statement that he is a Welshman. I mean, quite simply and ingenuously, that I know nothing about Wales—not even (for certain) that there is such a place. I went, indeed, a few weeks ago to a curious place full of rocks; and the people there *said* it was Wales. But, then, other people said that these people were very sly, and that you could not believe anything they said. But, then, as I did not believe the second people who did not believe the first people, it all came back to the same comfortable condition as before, which is one of blank and disinterested nescience. It is a condition I am in with regard to a large number of things in this world. I keep my faith for the things of another world. About this world I am a complete agnostic.

But in this particular case of ignorance I rather fancy that I am not alone. I think that the great majority of Englishmen have no real notion of the Welsh type or spirit, whatever it is. They have conceptions of the Scot and the Irishman, false conceptions, but always containing some lines of a true tradition. The Englishman does, so to speak, understand the Scotchman even when he misunderstands him. The Englishman does know what the Irish are, even while he demands indignantly of heaven why they are. The stingy Puritan in plaid trousers is a very crude and unjust version of that queer blend that makes the Scot—the combination of a certain coarseness of fibre with great intellectual keenness for abstract and even mystical things. Still, it is a version; the prose and poetry of the Scot remain in the caricature. The picture of Paddy at Donnybrook leaves out all the subtlety and self-tormenting irony that are mixed up with the pugnacity of the Irish. Still, the Irish are pugnacious; the Englishman has got the leading feature right. He knows that, for all his economics, the Scotchman often has a bee in his bonnet, and he knows that the Irishman generally has a wasp in his—a thing that will sting itself or anyone else merely for fun or glory.

In these cases, the caricature, though stiff, highly coloured, antiquated, and largely false, tells the remains of several truths. But who on earth has ever seen a caricature of a Welshman? In *Punch* and such papers we never see anything but pictures of a Welshwoman—as if there were no males in that peculiar country with the rocks. Even the woman is only marked as Welsh by wearing an extraordinary costume, rather like that of Cinderella's supernatural godmother. Without the artist suggesting any costume at all, one would recognize the very silly portraits of Irishmen with long upper lips, in the style of apes. Without any plaid trousers to assist the mind, one could spot the stiff beards and rocky cheek-bones of the Scotchmen of Charles Keene. But if you took away the Welshwoman's extraordinary hat, there would be nothing whatever to show that she was a Welshwoman. We have not in our minds a Welsh type to make fun of. It is interesting to remember that apparently Shakespeare had.

This state of entire non-understanding (as distinct from misunderstanding) of the Welsh seems to me just now to be not only unique, but important and rather serious. For, unless I am very much mistaken, Wales is going to play some peculiar, and perhaps dominant, part in the developments of our extraordinary time. If the Welsh begin to influence us without our having yet even begun to imagine them, we shall have the whole Irish business over again; the gradual or imperfect understanding of a thing in the process of wrestling with it in the dark. The indications of such a movement in Wales (wherever it is), the suggestion of the growing influence of Welshmen (whoever they may be), is something that comes to us rather by widely distributed happenings and hints than in any theatrical example. Some, however, would call Mr. Lloyd George a theatrical example; he has been called even more extraordinary things. And in that degree the thing is true. Mr. Lloyd George is very much more genuine and sincere and formidable in his capacity as leader of the little Welsh nation than he is in any of the other capacities in which he is foolishly praised and ridiculously reviled. But to anyone who really has an eye for history in action, the smallest strike secretary in a Welsh railway or colliery bulks much bigger in the present picture than Mr. Lloyd George. And it has been in Wales that many of the most dramatic and effective labour revolts have happened: above all it was in Wales that they presented peculiar features of their own, bad or good, which marked them out from the whole temper and habit of England in recent times. The modern theory of animals was challenged in the episode of the ponies in the mines. The modern theory of Jews was challenged in the violent Anti-Semite riots of the last few weeks. Things fierce and unfamiliar, things lost since the Middle Ages, are coming upon us out of the West.

As the curious incident of the quarrels between Welshmen and Jews has been mentioned, I will take the opportunity here of correcting a curious mistake that clings to the minds of numbers of my correspondents. There is in particular a gloomy gentleman in America who keeps on asking me how my Anti-Semite prejudice is getting on, and generally displaying a curiosity about how many Hebrew teeth I have pulled out this week, and how often a Pogrom is held in front of my house. He appears to base it all on some statement of mine that Jews were tyrants and traitors. Upon this basis his indignation is eloquent, lengthy and (in my opinion) just. The only weakness affecting this superstructure is the curious detail that I never did say that Jews were tyrants and traitors. I said that a particular kind of Jew tended to be a tyrant and another particular kind of Jew tended to be a traitor. I say it again. Patent facts of this kind are permitted in the criticism of every other nation on the planet: it is not counted illiberal to say that a certain kind of Frenchman tends to be sensual. It is as plain as a pikestaff that the Parisian tradition of life and letters has a marked element of sensuality. It is also as plain as a pikestaff that those who are creditors will always have a temptation to be tyrants, and that those who are cosmopolitans will always have a temptation to be spies. This has nothing to do with alleging that the majority of any people falls into its typical temptations. In this respect I should imagine that Jews varied in their moral proportions as much as the rest of mankind. Rehoboam was a tyrant; Jehoshaphat was not. In what is perhaps the most celebrated collection of Jews in human history, the proportion of traitors was one in twelve. But I cannot see why the tyrants should not be called tyrants and the traitors traitors; why Rehoboam should not cause a rebellion or Judas become an object of dislike, merely because they happen to be members of a race persecuted for other reasons and on other occasions. Those are my views on Jews. They are more reasonable than those of the people that wreck their shops; and much more reasonable than those of the people who justify them on all occasions.

"Ego et Shavius Meus"

ACCIDENT has cut me off this week from many current publications; and left me much to my own devices. It is therefore my immutable purpose to write an article about myself, under the thin pretence of noticing a book about Mr. Bernard Shaw.

This is all the more fun because it is exactly what Mr. Bernard Shaw would do himself; nor should I blame him. I like Mr. Shaw's type of Egoism; because, if he talks big, it is at least about big things; things bound to be bigger than himself.

I revolt, not against the loud egoist, but the gentle egoist; who talks tenderly of trifles; who says, "A sunbeam gilds the amber of my cigarette-holder; I find I cannot live without a cigarette-holder." I resist this arrogance simply because it is more arrogant. For even so complete a fool cannot really suppose we are interested in his cigarette-holder; and therefore must suppose that we are interested in him. But I defend a dogmatic egoist precisely because he deals in dogmas.

The Apostles' Creed is not regarded as a pose of foppish vanity; yet the word "I" comes before even the word "God." The believer comes first; but he is soon dwarfed by his beliefs, swallowed in the creative whirlwind and the trumpets of the resurrection. And if a man says he believes in the Superman or the Socialist State, I think him equally modest; only not so sensible.

Mr. Herbert Skimpole's book, *Bernard Shaw: the Man and His Work*, contains many suggestive and valuable things to which I cannot do justice, including allusions to myself mostly only too flattering, and in one case both amusing and mystifying. The passage suggests that all the active figures in my idle fictions are made as fat as I am; though I cannot recall that any of them are fat at all; except a semi-supernatural monster in a nightmare called *The Man Who Was Thursday*.

Let there be no alarm, however, that I shall talk about such nightmares, or any of my own tales; like Shaw, I am egoistic about things that matter. Mr. Skimpole says that while Shaw and I agree that the world should be adapted to the man, "Chesterton includes our present institutions among the parts of a man's soul which cannot be altered." Now there is here a potential mistake, which I will not apologize for taking more seriously than any fancy about the figures in my very amateurish romances.

I need not say I do not mind being called fat; for deprived of that jest, I should be almost a serious writer. I do not even mind being supposed to mind being called fat. But being supposed to be contented, and contented with the present institutions of modern society, is a mortal slander I will not take from any man.

Whatever are the institutions I defend, they are not primarily those of the present. They have been attempted in the past; and I hope they may be achieved in the future; but they are not present, but conspicuous by their absence. Mr. Skimpole truly says that I defend domesticity and piety and patriotism, but these are not the typical institutions of to-day.

The typical institutions of to-day are a Divorce Court cutting up families with the speed of a sausage machine; a Science which preaches the destiny without the divinity of Calvinism; and a Finance that crosses all frontiers with the same enlightened indifference that is shown by cholera.

These are the institutions of the instant, and even Mr. Skimpole has realized them as those of the immediate future. In a somewhat innocent passage he says that "it is of no use for Shaw to point out" to me the hope of a cosmopolitan future; "that Internationalism, social class-feeling, and Imperialism all point the same way he refuses to see."

It is indeed useless for Shaw to point out to me that I should follow the lead of these things; since I happen to detest Imperialism, disbelieve in Internationalism and distrust "social class-feeling," so far as I know what it means. I am well aware that an Imperial Chancellor in Berlin, an international money-lender in Johannesburg, and an anarchist spy in Petrograd, are "all pointing the same way"; and that is why I feel pretty safe in going the other.

I warmly apologize to Mr. Skimpole for writing a personal explanation instead of a review of his book, which contains many things well worth writing and reviewing; notably the shrewd remark about Shaw's style; in which what is a paradox in spirit is seldom an epigram in form. It takes our breath away rather by taking itself for granted than by defining itself like a defiance. But I fancy Mr. Skimpole will sympathize with me if

I am primarily concerned with his convictions, as he is with mine, and as we both are with Shaw's.

And he has gone to the vital point in emphasizing this matter of the things permanent in man. When I say that religion and marriage and local loyalty are permanent in humanity, I mean that they recur when humanity is most human; and only comparatively decline when society is comparatively inhuman.

They have declined in the modern world. They may return through the war; but anyhow, where we have the small farm and the free man and the fighting spirit, there we shall have the salute to the soil and the roof and to the altar.

To take a more casual case: I believe that when men are happy, they sing; not only at the piano but at the plough, or at least in the intervals of ploughing; at their work and in their walks abroad. I am well aware that modern men do not sing in the street very much. I am well aware that cosmopolitan money-lenders never sing, but die with all their music in them. I know that the Song of the Happy Meat-Contractor is not one of "our present institutions."

I know that one can seldom come at dawn upon some solitary London banker carolling more sweetly than the lark; and even his clerks do not often sing in chorus over their ledgers. But I still think it is more human to sing than not to sing; and that, being more human, it is more permanent in humanity.

Some righteous revolution will teach the bankers and contractors that little birds who can sing and won't sing must be made to sing—or at any rate made to squeal. In the interlude, the instinct of song takes refuge in the lesser thing called poetry, or even prose; and to-morrow the fever of personal sincerity may have passed; and I shall return, with a lowly air, to literature.

The Plan for a New Universe

THERE is one theory of the Origin of Species which I have never seen suggested. Probably this is because I have never read the numberless and voluminous works in which it has been suggested. For I have read much madder things, and nothing mad is likely to have been missed by the modern mind. But since it shocked the respectability of agnostics to suggest that all creatures had been made different by God, why did nobody suggest that they had been made different by Man? Why not trace the vast variety of animals as we can really trace the vast variety of dogs? The dog is already almost a world in himself, with all the appearance of distinct orders and types. A St. Bernard approaches the size and surpasses the legendary virtues of a lion; while there is a sort of Pekinese which a man might almost tread on as a somewhat unpleasing insect. Yet all this world of evolution has presumably had Man for its god. Suppose our sphere in space has itself been the Island of Dr. Moreau. Suppose Man had some prehistoric civilization so colossal and complete that all beasts were beasts of burden, or all animals were domestic animals; that all rabbits were pet rabbits or all fleas performing fleas. Suppose the tame bird came first, and what we know as the wild bird afterwards. Mr. Bernard Shaw, in one of his early anti-domestic diatribes, compared a woman in the home to a parrot in the cage, saying that mere custom made us think the connexion natural. The answer, it has always seemed to me, is strangely obvious. It is surely plain that the housewife is not the bird in the cage, but the bird in the nest. But if, in that age of wild sceptics, anyone had wished to outdo Mr. Shaw in paradox, he could have done it brilliantly by this hypothesis that the colours of a parrot were actually produced in a cage; and that an exiled bird only built himself a rude den of sticks and mud as an outlaw does when driven from his home. Suppose, in short, that Man has not only been a dog-fancier, but a wolf-fancier and a hyena-fancier. Suppose he really fancied a rhinoceros. Suppose some prehistoric squire kept a stud of giraffes; or his money-lender got a peerage on the plea that he had improved the breed of crocodiles. Then we have only to suppose this universal Zoo broken up like the Roman Empire; and all we see is its neglect and riot. The tiger is a stray cat; a specially large and handsome cat who took the prize (and the prize-giver) and escaped to the jungle. A whale was some sort of hornless cow sent into the sea like a Newfoundland dog, who suddenly refused to come back again. This thesis accounts for the comparative rapidity of the differentiation, over which the geologists fight with the biologists. It accounts rationalistically for those evidences of a creative purpose which are so distressing to a refined mind. It accounts for the camel, who seems always to have been in captivity; and accounting for a camel is something. Above all, it accounts for that very vivid impression of something in various species at once outrageous and exact. Jefferies found in the farcical outlines of fish or bird the notion that they must have been produced without design. To me this sounds like saying that the caricatures of Max Beerbohm must have been produced without design. I could as easily believe, so far as this mere æsthetic impression goes, that the face on a gargoyle was merely moulded by the pouring rain. Artistically, the sun-fish or the hornbill do not look in the least like accidents; but it might be maintained that they look like fashions. There are some tropical birds and fruits that really have the cut and colours of novelties in a shop window. We might fancy that an elephant was designed in the same taste as Babylonian architecture; or the leopard and the tiger to match the tapestries of the East. There is probably somewhere a bird as sinister and terrifying as a top-hat; and in some luxuriant jungle a plant as preposterous as a pair of trousers. The monsters may be only antiquated fashion-plates. For this is one of the numberless neglected fallacies in the clotted folly of Eugenics. Even if we could in the abstract breed humanity well, there would be a flutter of modes and crazes about what was considered well-bred. The dog is bred with design; but surely not always with discretion. The dachshund appears to have been pulled out on the rack of some demoniac vivisectionist; and somebody seems to have cut off the bull-dog's nose, most emphatically to spite his face. On the analogy of the things we do breed, the Eugenist may be expected to produce a brood of hunchbacks or a pure race of Albinos.

It is, I hope, unnecessary to remark that I do not believe in this theory; but there have been people who might well have believed in it. There were people who could believe in Swinburne's sentiment, "Glory to Man in the highest; for Man is the master of things"; and it would surely have completed this consciousness in the poet if he could have thought that the birds of Putney Heath, where he walked, or the fishes in the sea, where he was so fond of swimming, were doing tricks taught to them as to performing dogs. Suppose that such a fancy had fitted in with one of the humanitarian religions of that time, how far would it have satisfied what was often called the religious sentiment? It would not have satisfied any religious sentiment, not even Swinburne's. He would have cared as little as Shelley to claim the birds when he could not claim the sky. He certainly would have been much annoyed with the notion of loving the fishes, if he were not allowed to go on loving the sea. And though he poisoned paganism with pessimism, a thing not only more false but more frivolous, though he tried to love the sea as a wanton or admire the sky as a tyrant, though this morbidity weakened his love of Nature not only as compared with Virgil or Dante, but as compared with Wordsworth or Whitman, yet he was like every poet elemental, and what he loved were the elementary things. And this is an essential of any poetry and any religion. It must appeal to the origins and deal with the first things, however much or little it may say about them. It must be at home in the homeless void, before the first star was made. The one thing every man knows about the unknowable is that it is the Indispensable.

Now, if any reader thinks that the scientific heresy I sketched above is too irrational for moderns to have held, I have the pleasure of informing him that moderns are now about to announce, or have already announced, a new heresy somewhat analogous but much less rationalistic and much less rational. There is a new religion; that is a new fault being found with the old religion. There is a new plan for a new universe, which may be expected to last for many a long month to come. It is the view that seems to have satisfied Mr. Wells, or, at any rate, Mr. Britling. It is the view which has been more than once suggested by Mr. Shaw, and is repeated in the skeleton of certain lectures he is delivering. It is much more supernatural and even superstitious than my imaginary thesis; for instead of giving to man more of the powers of God, it arbitrarily imagines a God and then limits him with the impotence of man. He is not limited, as in the theologies, by his own reason or justice or desire for the freedom of man. He is limited by unreason and injustice and the impossibility of freedom even for himself. But I do not make this note upon the new development with any intention of discussing it thoroughly in its theological aspect; though there is one aspect of that aspect which may respectfully be called amusing. When I was a boy, Christianity was blamed by the freethinkers for its anthropomorphic demigod, substituted by savages for the Unknown God who made all things. Now Christianity is blamed for the flat contrary; because its God is unknown and not anthropomorphic enough. Thirty years ago we only needed the First Person of the Trinity; and thirty years later we have discovered that we only need the Second. This sort of fashion-plate philosophy will no doubt go on as usual. In a few decades we may be told that our fathers were profoundly right when they believed in the Archangel Gabriel, but made an inexplicable mistake when they believed in the Archangel Raphael. We shall learn that the Seraphim are an exploded superstition, but the Cherubim a most valuable and novel discovery. And as my note is not concerned with the theological, neither is it directly concerned with the purely logical side of it. Here again, it seems obvious that all the doubts which legitimately attach to the idea of a progressive humanity are absolutely fatal to the idea of a progressive divinity. A man may be progressing towards God; but what is a God progressing towards? And how does he know which of two developments in consciousness is the better (*e.g.*, an imaginative compassion or an imaginative cruelty) if there be no aboriginal standard in his own nature? I am here only concerned to note the failure of this fancy where it is parallel to the failure of the fancy I mentioned first. And it is the weakness which would instantly be discovered in both of them, not only by every poet but by every child. It is that unless the sky is beautiful, nothing is beautiful. Unless the background of all things is good, it is no substitute to make the foreground better: it may be right to do so for other reasons, but not for the reason that is the root of religion. Materialism says the universe is mindless; and faith says it is ruled by the highest mind. Neither will be satisfied with the new progressive creed, which declares hopefully that the universe is half-witted.

George Wyndham

I BELIEVE more and more that there are no trivialities but only truths neglected; but the things I myself neglect accumulate in mountains. I have made a note of one of them found in turning over the recent files of the *Nation*. Elsewhere was a reminder about a book I had long admired and enjoyed, but which had been crowded out of my mind by less pleasant things; the book of recollections about George Wyndham, recently written by Mr. Charles Gatty and published by Mr. Murray.[1] Even now I cannot do justice to the book; but I know Mr. Gatty will approve of my saying a word to correct an injustice to the subject of the book.

Some time ago the *Nation* dismissed Mr. Gatty's volume, not with disrespect, but with a certain distance and indifference evidently founded on a very mistaken idea. It implied that Wyndham was after all an intellectual aristocrat, whose culture was that of a clique, and who did not test it enough in popular and practical politics. The point is interesting; chiefly because it is the precise reverse of the truth. If anything could narrow a man like Wyndham, it was being political like the *Nation*; what broadened him to a universal brotherhood was getting far from politics—like the nation. His private life was much larger than his public life; though that in turn was larger than most public lives in the parliamentary decline. Being a politician, he had to be a parliamentarian; and being a parliamentarian, he had to be an oligarch. In so far as he did hold the aristocratic theory, it was exactly that aristocratic theory that forced him into political practice. He knew well enough, I think, that the English parliament is an aristocracy. He took the high ground of the responsibility of privilege; but he was far too sincere to deny that it was privilege. He said to a friend of mine, who thus lamented his laborious parliamentary botherations, "You see, I was born paid." It was the aristocracy the *Nation* reproves that necessitated the parliamentarism the *Nation* desires or demands. Personally, I should not desire either; and I think the real Wyndham was in a larger world outside both. It was precisely where he was most domestic that he was most

---

[1] *George Wyndham: Recognita*, by C. T. Gatty. Murray. 7s. 6d. net.

democratic. He was a poet among poets exactly as he might have been a pedestrian among pedestrians or, as he would have preferred to put it, a tramp among tramps. The sympathy with tramps might be taken literally; for I remember him defending the gipsies, when a more modern spirit wanted them taught the meaning of progress by being moved on by the police. He may have been right to work in cabinets and committees; but it was there, if anywhere, that he was in a clique. He may have been right not to follow his tastes, but it was his tastes that were popular and what many cliques would call vulgar. He may have been right not to be one of the idle rich, but he might have been even more superior to the limits of the rich, if he had been idler.

The beauty of Mr. Gatty's book is that it is a brilliant scrap-book, the very variegated nature of which expresses this almost vagabond liberality. Even when it merely notes down such things as single lines of Shakespeare over which Wyndham lingered, or reproduces corners of carving or painting which arrested his eye, the method seems to me to work rightly; it seems somehow natural to talk of every other subject besides the subject himself; as he was always ready to talk of every other subject. And this aspect, by itself, accentuates the feeling that his holidays were his most useful days. In this mood one may well wish that he had never been near what he himself called the cesspool of politics; and one might well accept the *Nation's* suggestion of his aloofness from its own favourite parliamentary business with a somewhat dry assent. Wyndham certainly had little to do with the internal constructive legislation praised in progressive papers. He can claim none of the glory of the great social reforms of the period just before the War. He is not responsible for the permission to drag away a poor man's child as a raving maniac, if his teacher thinks he is a little too stupid to learn, or his teacher is a little too stupid to teach him. He has not the honour of having abolished the Habeas Corpus Act, in order to allow amateur criminologists to keep a tramp in prison until they have invented a science of criminology. He did not establish the Labour Exchanges, and probably did not want to establish them, any more than the Labour Exchanges vividly described in *Uncle Tom's Cabin*. It was not he who created by statute a servant class, of men made to spend their own wages on doctors they might never want, instead of on tools or tram-tickets they urgently wanted. He was largely detached from all this; and when reading a real record like Mr. Gatty's one is moved to wish that he had been even more detached from it. Considering the liberty of his philosophical friendships, one respects but regrets the loyalty of his political friendships; and is sorry that common sense must be sacrificed to practical politics.

But when a book like Mr. Gatty's has moved a reviewer to this mood of mere regret for a poet wasted in politics, there returns upon him after all one answer which is itself unanswerable. Judged by one ultimate test, he was after all right to remain in politics; even in the last putrefaction of parliamentary politics. At the price of nobody knows what pain and patience and contempt and concessions, he alone among modern politicians did leave not merely a name but a thing, that will remain after him as a scientific engine or a geographical discovery remains. He achieved a work which has changed the whole destiny of Western Europe; the resurrection of Ireland. There he established the free peasant; a work organically different from all the modern reforms that are merely imposed, whether right or wrong, whether servile or socialist. It is the difference between planting a tree and building a tower; once planted, the tree lives by its own life. He and his admirers, myself among the number, might well be content to contemplate such a work without afterthoughts; if there were not laid upon us like a load of memories, and almost like a living chain, the love of England.

For England, alas! has made to-day the worst possible compromise between aristocracy and democracy. It has kept the aristocracy and lost the aristocrats. The country is still as much ruled by squires, but not so much by country gentlemen; and the reform of the House of Lords seems to mean eliminating gentlemen and carefully preserving noblemen. It is as if there were a complaint of martial law; and it were met by keeping the whole machinery of militarism, but giving the arbitrary power to spies instead of soldiers. Or it is as if reactionaries erected a despotism, and then called themselves reformers because they did not care what dirty fellow was despot. But remote as Wyndham was from the sham gentry of the twentieth century, it would also be an error merely to merge him with the genuine gentry of the eighteenth. It would be to mark the type so as to miss the man. What distinguished him, as an individual, from good and bad squires, was something far older than squirarchy; the true sense of the squire expectant, eager to spring into the saddle of knighthood. His courage was far less static than that of a country gentleman. It was the thing in which a philologist might recognize that "courage" really means rushing; or from which a professor will probably some day prove that courage really means running away. He had that spiritual ambition which is itself the ascending flame of humility; and which has been wanting to the English since the squire grew greater than the knight. He seemed to await an adventure that never quite came to him on earth; and his life and death were swift, as if he were struck by lightning as with an accolade, or had won spurs that were wings upon the wind.

Four Stupidities

I HAVE just seen a newspaper paragraph which, whether it refers to a fact or merely a suggestion, seems to me to go down pretty well into that depth of mindlessness which calls itself the modern mind. It is said that influence is being brought to bear on the American Government to induce them to break a bottle of water instead of a bottle of champagne when they christen a battleship. Now it is not easy to deal adequately with the rich stupidity of that. It is about five follies thick, stupidity obscuring stupidity until one reader can hardly see more than one of the jokes at a time. There is something almost fascinating in the idea of trying to disentangle them.

First Stupidity. Note the notion that there is something so intrinsically and supernaturally evil about an intoxicant that the pure temperance man will not touch it even when it cannot intoxicate anybody. It is as if a man were to insist on having a teetotal boot-polish or a teetotal printing-ink. A cup of tea, or even of hot milk, becomes diabolic if you have boiled the kettle with methylated spirit. Eau-de-Cologne is a blackguard indulgence, though you use it only to scent your handkerchief. A liquor containing alcohol (such as ginger-beer) is simply and superstitiously an accursed thing, which is not only not to be touched with the lips, but not to be touched with the hands. After this case, the more intemperate "Temperance" people cannot pretend any longer that their proposal is merely a social reform; it is obviously and literally a mystical taboo. I do not see what right such people have to mock at the savage's fear of a fetish, still less at the peasant's respect for the relic of a saint. There might surely be such a thing as holy water, if it be so certain that there is such a thing as unholy water.

Second Stupidity. The extraordinary confusion by which it becomes not only wicked to possess wine (though you never drink it), but becomes wicked even to destroy it. This goes, I think, much further than this queer materialist madness has yet gone. If a champagne bottle is smashed to smithereens over the prow of a ship, I should have thought the most logical teetotaller would merely have been glad that there was one champagne bottle less in the world. As he would probably not be a person with any special sympathy with the old ceremonials of revelry, that is the only possible way in which I can imagine the thing affecting him. We in England used to think we could trace a slight streak of fanaticism in good Mrs. Carrie Nation, who used to go about breaking other people's wine and spirit bottles with her little hatchet. But now it would appear that Mrs. Carrie Nation was a wobbler, one weakly compromising with the fiend of fermented drink, perhaps nobbled by the Liquor Trade—or, worse still, verging on the loathly state of a moderate drinker. She ought to have been summoned before a tribunal of these New Teetotallers and condemned for ever having gone near enough to a bottle to touch it, even with a hatchet; condemned for having so much as hung about the hellish tavern, where the very fumes of its fiery poisons might have mounted to her head. The principle is an interesting one, and might be extended to many cases. Thus, when the common hangman burned a book of treason or heresy, he may be supposed to have been infected by the intellectual errors it contained. Thus when a censor blacks out a paragraph in a newspaper, he may be held to have sinned even in looking to see where the paragraph was. This, apparently, is the new barbaric fancy: that certain vegetable drinks are so demonic that we not only are wrong when we drink them, but are wrong when we do our best to render them undrinkable.

Third Stupidity. The curious deadness of the mind in such men is illustrated at the next stage; that of clinging convulsively to a mere form; and not only not knowing, but not so much as wondering—first, whether the idea is worth preserving; and, secondly, whether they are preserving it. The mark of this dead and broken traditionalism is always two-fold. It can be seen in these two facts: that men alter a thing as if it had no sense in it; and yet they never have the sense to abolish what is for them a senseless thing. I can see much dignity in absolute austerity and the refusal of symbol; I can see some dignity even in dingy utilitarianism and the refusal of art. I could respect the perfect plainness of an early Quaker like Penn when he would not take his hat off in the palace, because it was an idle form. I do not despise him because he came afterwards (I believe) to see that keeping your hat on is just as much of a form as taking it off; and took off his hat like other people. But if Penn had strictly confined himself, say, to taking off his hatband with laborious care, every time he entered the Royal presence, I should say that he had lost both his Quakerism and his sociability. He would have lost the independence that refuses recognition to the world, and he would not have gained the disputable substitute of good manners. Similarly, I could respect (though I could not envy) the flinty old Manchester manufacturers who regarded all expenditure on arms, especially on drums, flags, or trumpets, as so much babyish waste of money. But I should not even have respected them if they had proposed that the British Army should fly the White Flag in every battle because it was cheaper than a coloured one. Why have a flag at all, if it comes to that? Or, again, I can understand the unconverted Scrooge with his bowl of gruel; and I like the converted Scrooge with his bowl of punch. But if Scrooge had insisted every Christmas on having a punch-bowl with no punch in it, I should not understand at all.

Fourth Stupidity. Besides this general deadness, there is a strange special deadness to the human sentiment behind that special sort of ceremony. Don't express the sentiment if you think it a silly sentiment; but don't so express it as to prove that you haven't got it. That sentiment is the ancient sentiment of sacrifice. The thing sacrificed may be anything: wine, as on the battleship; gold, as when the Doge threw his ring into the sea; an ox or a sheep, as among the ancient pagans; and very occasionally, when tribes savage or civilized are seized with Satanist panic, a man. But it must be something *valuable*, or the particular thrill, wholesome or unwholesome, is not obtained. It was generally the best sheep or the best ox; and in the rare cases of human sacrifice, generally somebody like the King's daughter. Like all human appetites, it is both good and evil; it has many roots, a gesture of generosity, an appeal to the unknown, a guarantee against arrogance, a dim idea of not taking all one's advantage from fortune: but they all depend on the *value*, and these men evidently understand none of them, when they fill the bottle with water.

On Historical Novels

IT is very easy, of course, to smile at such schoolboy fiction as the novels of Mr. Henty, in which the same very English and modern young gentleman from Rugby or Harrow turns up again and again as a Young Greek, a Young Carthaginian, a Young Scandinavian, a Young Gaul, a Young Visigoth, a Young Ancient Briton, and almost everything short of a Young Negro. But Mr. Henty had the merits of his industry and fecundity; and one of them was that he did take a boy's imagination into many and varied parts of human history, however conventional the figure he followed through them might be. The English boy will not find out as much about the soul of Carthage from the *Young Carthaginian* as a lover of letters may from *Salammbô*; but at least he will know that Carthage was conquered—and that is (for various reasons) a good thing for English people to know. And since the Henty period our historical novels have fallen with terrible sameness into two or three grooves. We might almost say that a man is not allowed to write an historical novel except about four different historical periods, about six different historical characters; and even about them he is not allowed to take any view except that taken by the other romances on the same subject. Now, considering the countless millions of marvellous, amusing, unique, and picturesque things that have thronged on top of each other through all our wonderful three thousand years of European history, this state of affairs is as Byzantine and benighted as if no landscape painter ever painted anything but a larch tree, or as if none of our sculptors could model anything except the left leg.

You may write a novel about the time of Henry of Navarre—in fact, it might almost be said that you must write a novel about the time of Henry of Navarre. If you go in for writing historical novels at all, somebody—the publisher or the office-boy—makes you do this. In this novel, Huguenots must be gallant gentlemen, with a touch of bluffness; Catholics must also be gallant gentlemen, with a touch of slyness. All important political questions must be settled by duels fought with long rapiers at wayside inns. You must stick to one side of the quarrel; but even in that you must not bring any of the charges that a person of the period might really have brought. For instance, the Court must be perpetually engaged in plotting to stab the bluff Huguenot: but you must not insist that the Huguenot was a Puritan, and his objection to the Court would largely be that it was a Renaissance Court. You must not, however delicately, bring in that presence of florid pagan sensuality and princely indecorum which we feel in Brantome or the Tales of the Queen of Navarre. The Latins must stick to assassination. There must be no people to speak of in Paris, though it was the people of Paris who, for good or evil, changed the whole course of the history. Men like Sully may be introduced; but their talents must be entirely occupied in serving the Prince in his personal love-affairs and in his duels in inns. Above all, slap in the very middle of the Wars of Religion, nobody must seem to have any clear idea of what his own religion is about. You may also write a novel about the time of Richelieu. But it must be governed by the same principles. Richelieu must be a sinister yet magnanimous enemy of the hero. He must try to kill the hero, and unaccountably fail. At this stage of the writing of historical novels, it is important to be an imitator of Dumas. There are critics who maintain that Dumas was largely written by imitators of Dumas. This is an exaggeration; but, at the worst, they were good imitators. There are chapters in the triple tale of the Musketeers of which I can only say that, if anyone but he wrote them, he could hire hearts and heads as well as hands. But my warning to the young writer of entirely useless historical novels is this: He must not go outside France, or treat that country otherwise than as an insulated elfland. He must not carry off General Monk in a box. Think what a frightful mistake would have been made—from the English Puritan point of view—if d'Artagnan had carried off General Cromwell by mistake! All this happened in the time of Mazarin and not Richelieu, but the principle will be found reliable. The principle is that neither Richelieu nor anybody else should show the faintest interest in the future of France.

You may write a novel about the French Revolution. You may do it on your head, as the jolly habitual criminals say. The essential principles of this sort of novel are: (1) That the populace of Paris from 1790 to 1794 never had any meals, nor even sat down in a café. They stood about in the street all night and all day, sufficiently sustained by the sight of Blood, especially Blue Blood. (2) All power during the Terror was in the hands of the public executioner and of Robespierre; and these persons were subject to abrupt changes of mind, and frequently redeemed their habit of killing people for no apparent reason by letting them off at the last moment, for no apparent reason either. (3) Aristocrats are of two kinds—the very wicked and the entirely blameless; and both are invariably good-looking. Both also appear rather to prefer being guillotined. (4) Such things as the invasion of France, the idea of a Republic, the influence of Rousseau, the nearness of national bankruptcy, the work of Carnot with the armies, the policy of Pitt, the policy of Austria, the ineradicable habit of protecting one's property against foreigners, and the presence of persons carrying guns at the Battle of Valmy—all these things had nothing to do with the French Revolution, and should be omitted.

Now, considering the number of picturesque struggles there have been in the world, it seems to me that these subjects might be given a rest. There has been next to nothing written, for instance, about the other Wars of Religion, those that accompanied the construction of Catholic Europe, rather than its breaking up. There was the Iconoclast invasion of Italy, which ends with the entrance of Charlemagne. There has been next to nothing written about riots other than the Parisian; the many riots of Edinburgh, especially of those few days when it was almost as dangerous to be a doctor as to be a mad dog. Another advantage would be that, coming fresh to his historical problem, the writer might even read a little history.

On Monsters

I ONCE saw in the newspapers this paragraph, of which I made a note:

"LEPRECHAUN" CAUGHT

Great excitement has been caused in Mullingar, in the west of Ireland, by the report that the supposed "Leprechaun," which several children stated they had seen at Killough, near Delvin, during the past two months, was captured. Two policemen found a creature of dwarfish proportions in a wood near the town, and brought the little man to Mullingar Workhouse, where he is now an inmate. He eats greedily, but all attempts to interview him have failed, his only reply being a peculiar sound between a growl and a squeal. The inmates regard him with interest mixed with awe.

This seems like the beginning of an important era of research; it seems as if the world of experiments had at last touched the world of reality. It is as if one read: "Great excitement has been caused in Rotten Row, in the west of London, by the fact that the centaur, previously seen by several colonels and young ladies, has at last been stopped in his lawless gallop." Or it is as if one saw in a newspaper: "Slight perturbation has been caused at the west end of Margate by the capture of a mermaid," or "A daring fowler, climbing the crags of the Black Mountains for a nest of eagles, found, somewhat unexpectedly, that it was a nest of angels." It is wonderful to have the calm admission in cold print of such links between the human world and other worlds. It is interesting to know that they took the Leprechaun to a workhouse. It settles, and settles with a very sound instinct, the claim of humanity in such sublime curiosities. If a centaur were really found in Rotten Row, would they take him to a workhouse or to a stable? If a mermaid were really fished up at Margate, would they take her to a workhouse or to an aquarium? If people caught an angel unawares, would they put the angel in a workhouse? Or in an aviary?

The idea of the Missing Link was not at all new with Darwin; it was not invented merely by those vague but imaginative minor poets to whom we owe most of our ideas about evolution. Men had always played about with the idea of a possible link between human and bestial life; and the very existence—or, if you will, the very non-existence—of the centaur or the mermaid proves it. All the mythologies had dreamed of a half-human monster. The only objection to the centaur and the mermaid was that they could not be found. In every other respect their merits were of the most solid sort. So it is with the Darwinian ideal of a link between man and the brutes. There is no objection to it except that there is no evidence for it. The only objection to the Missing Link is that he is apparently fabulous, like the centaur and the mermaid, and all the other images under which man has imagined a bridge between himself and brutality. In short, the only objection to the Missing Link is that he is missing.

But there is also another very elementary difference. The Greeks and the Mediævals invented monstrosities. But they treated them as monstrosities—that is, they treated them as exceptions. They did not deduce any law from such lawless things as the centaur or the merman, the griffin or the hippogriff. But modern people did try to make a law out of the Missing Link. They made him a lawgiver, though they were hunting for him like a criminal. They built on the foundation of him before he was found. They made this unknown monster, the mixture of the man and ape, the founder of society and the accepted father of mankind. The ancients had a fancy that there was a mongrel of horse and man, a mongrel of fish and man. But they did not make it the father of anything; they did not ask the mad mongrel to breed. The ancients did not draw up a system of ethics based upon the centaur, showing how man in a civilized society must take care of his hands, but must not wholly forget his hooves. They never reminded woman that, although she had the golden hair of a goddess, she had the tail of a fish. But the moderns did talk to man as if he were the Missing Link; they did remind him that he must allow for apish imbecility and bestial tricks. The moderns did tell the woman that she was half a brute, for all her beauty; you can find the thing said again and again in Schopenhauer and other prophets of the modern spirit. That is the real difference between the two monsters. The Missing Link is still missing and so is the merman. On the top of all this we have the Leprechaun, apparently an actual monster at present in the charge of the police. It is unnecessary to say that numbers of learned people have proved again and again that it could not exist. It is equally unnecessary to say that numbers of unlearned people—children, mothers of children, workers, common people who grow corn or catch fish—had seen them existing. Almost every other simple type of our working population had seen a Leprechaun. A fisherman had seen a Leprechaun. A farmer had seen a Leprechaun. Even a postman had probably seen one. But there was one simple son of the people whose path had never before been crossed by the prodigy. Never until then had a policeman seen a Leprechaun. It was only a question of whether the monster should take the policeman away with him into Elfland (where such a policeman as he would certainly have been fettered by the fatal love of the fairy queen), or whether the policeman should take away the monster to the police-station. The forces of this earth prevailed; the constable captured the elf, instead of the elf capturing the constable. The officer took him to the workhouse, and opened a new epoch in the study of tradition and folk-lore.

What will the modern world do if it finds (as very likely it will) that the wildest fables have had a basis in fact; that there are creatures of the border land, that there are oddities on the fringe of fixed laws, that there are things so unnatural as easily to be called preternatural? I do not know what the modern world will do about these things; I only know what I hope. I hope the modern world will be as sane about these things as the mediæval world was about them. Because I believe that an ogre can have two heads, that is no reason why I should lose the only head that I have. Because the mediæval man thought that some man had the head of a dog, that was no reason why he himself should have the head of a donkey. The mediæval man was never essentially weak or stupid about any of his beliefs, however unfounded they were. He did not lack judgment; he only lacked the opportunities of judgment. He had superstitions; but he was not superstitious about them. He was wrong about Africa; but then, to do him justice, he did not care whether he was right. He had got that particular thing which some modern people call "the love of truth," but which is really simply the power of taking one's own mistakes seriously. He thought that ordinary men were a serious matter; as they are. He thought that extraordinary men were a fantastic fairy-tale; and he thought (very rightly) that the fairy-tale was all the more fantastic if it was true. He did not let dog-faced men affect his conception of mankind; he regarded them as a joke, the best as a practical joke. But in our time, I am sorry to say, we have seen some signs of the possibility that such aberrations or monstrosities as spiritual science may discover will be taken as real tests of, or keys to, the human lot. For instance, the psychological phenomenon called "dual personality" is certainly a thing so extraordinary that any old-fashioned rationalist or agnostic would simply have called it a miracle and disbelieved it. But nowadays those who do believe it will not treat it as a miracle— that is, as an exception. They try to make deductions from it, theories about identity and metempsychosis and psychical evolution, and God knows what. If it is true that one particular body has two souls, it is a joke, as if it had two noses. It must not be permitted to upset the actualities of our human happiness. If some one says, "Jones blew his nose," and Jones is of so peculiar a formation that one may with logical propriety ask, "Which nose?" that is no reason why the ordinary formula should lose its ordinary human utility. This is, I think, one of the most real dangers that lie in front of the civilization that has just discovered the Leprechaun. We are going to find all the gods and fairies all over again, all the spiritual hybrids and all the jests of eternity. But we are not going to find them, as the pagans found them, in our youth, in an atmosphere in which gods can be jested with or giants slapped on the back. We are going to find them, in the old age of our society, in a mood dangerously morbid, in a spirit only too ready to take the exception instead of the rule. If we find creatures that are half human, we may only too possibly make them an excuse for being half-human ourselves. I should not be very painfully concerned about the Leprechaun if people had thrown stones at him as a bad fairy, or given him milk and fire as a good one. But there is something menacing about taking away a monster in order to study him. There is something sinister about putting a Leprechaun in the workhouse. The only solid comfort is that he certainly will not work.